PRENTICE-HALL FOUNDATIONS OF MODERN PSYCHOLOGY SERIES

Richard S. Lazarus, Editor

The Psychological Development of the Child, 3rd ed., Paul Mussen

Tests and Measurements, 3rd ed., Leona E. Tyler and W. Bruce Walsh

Personality, 3rd ed., Richard S. Lazarus and Alan Monat

Clinical Psychology, 2nd ed., Julian B. Rotter

Perception, 2nd ed., Julian E. Hochberg

Learning, 2nd ed., Sarnoff A. Mednick, Howard R. Pollio, and Elizabeth F. Loftus

Social Psychology, 2nd ed., William W. Lambert and Wallace E. Lambert

Organizational Psychology, 2nd ed., Edgar H. Schein

Abnormal Psychology, Sheldon Cashdan

Humanistic Psychology, John B. P. Shaffer

School Psychology, Jack I. Bardon and Virginia C. Bennett

LEONA E. TYLER

W. BRUCE WALSH
Ohio State University

Tests
and
Measurements
3rd edition

PRENTICE-HALL, INC., Englewood Cliffs, New Jersey 07632

Library of Congress Cataloging in Publication Data

Tyler, Leona Elizabeth,
  Tests and measurements.

  (Foundations of modern psychology series)
  Bibliography: p.
  Includes index.
  1. Psychological tests. 2. Psychometrics.
I.   Walsh, W. Bruce,   joint author.
II.   Title.
BF39.T9 1979   150'.28   78-23772
ISBN 0-13-911859-4
ISBN 0-13-911842-X pbk.

Foundation of Modern Psychology Series
Richard S. Lazarus, Editor

Printed in the United States of America

10 9 8 7 6 5 4 3 2 1

Editorial/production supervision by
Cathie Mick Mahar
Interior design and cover design by
Virginia M. Soulé
Manufacturing buyer:
Phil Galea

Prentice-Hall International, Inc., London
Prentice-hall of Australia Pty. Limited, Sydney
Prentice-Hall of Canada, Ltd., Toronto
Prentice-Hall of India Private Limited, New Delhi
Prentice-Hall of Japan, Inc., Tokyo
Prentice-Hall of Southeast Asia Pte. Ltd., Singapore
Whitehall Books Limited, Wellington, New Zealand

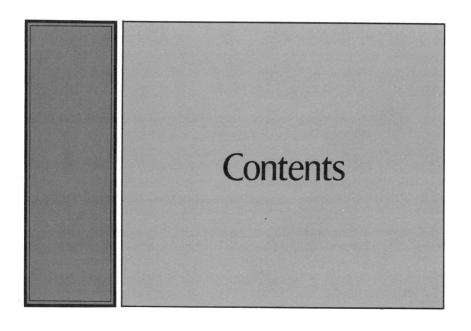

Contents

v

6

PERSONALITY ASSESSMENT
75

7

VOCATIONAL PSYCHOLOGY AND ASSESSMENT
104

8

APPLICATION OF
TESTS AND MEASUREMENTS
120

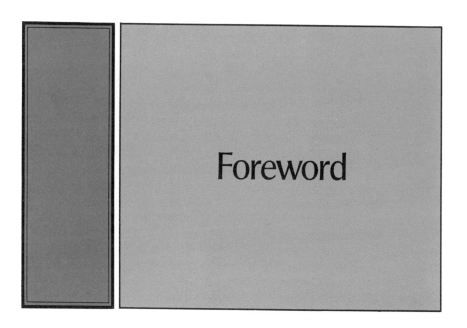

Foreword

The Foundations of Modern Psychology Series was the first and most successful in what became a trend in psychology toward groups of short texts dealing with various basic subjects, each written by an active authority. It was conceived with the idea of providing greater flexibility for instructors teaching general courses than was ordinarily available in the large, encyclopedic textbooks, and greater depth of presentation for individual topics not typically given much space in introductory textbooks.

The earliest volumes appeared in 1963, the latest in 1978 with the continuing expansion of the series into new areas of psychology. They are in widespread use as supplementary texts, or as the text, in various undergraduate courses in psychology. education, public health, sociology, and social work; and clusters of volumes have served as textbooks for undergraduate courses in general psychology. Groups of volumes have been translated into many languages including Danish, Dutch, Finnish, French, German, Hebrew, Italian, Japanese, Malaysian, Norwegian, Polish, Portuguese, Spanish, and Swedish.

With wide variation in publication date and type of content, some of the volumes have needed revision, while others have not. We have left this decision to the individual author. Some have remained unchanged, some have been modestly changed and updated, and still others completely rewritten. We have also opted for variation in length and style to reflect the different ways in which they have been used as texts.

There has never been stronger interest in good teaching in our colleges and universities than there is now; and for this the availability of high quality, well-written, and stimulating text materials highlighting the exciting and continuing search for knowledge is a prime requisite. This is especially the case in undergraduate courses where large numbers of students must have access to suitable readings. The Foundations of Modern Psychology Series represents an ongoing attempt to provide college teachers with the most authoritative and flexible textbook materials we can create.

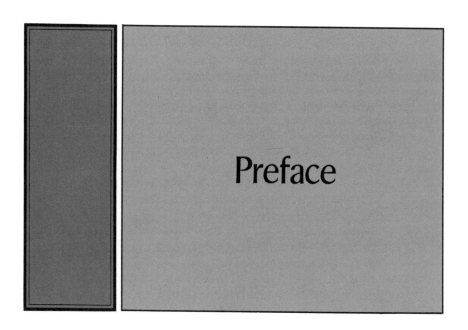

Preface

In this third revision of *Tests and Measurements* we have up-dated certain content areas, expanded others, and added one chapter in an effort to make the book more meaningful and useful for teachers, practitioners, and students in the field. The most profound change centers about the addition of a new chapter entitled Vocational Psychology and Assessment. This chapter focuses on the field of vocational psychology as it reflects the convergence of theory, assessment, and research. Thus, selected theories of career development are reviewed that have implication for assessment and practical application. We thought that this new information would not only tend to integrate psychological assessment and vocational psychology, but, in addition, would help students organize and understand data about themselves and their social environments.

There have been many new *variations*, new statistical techniques, new tests, new standardizations of old ones, but few changes in concepts or principles. The dramatic increases in the size, sophistication, and general utilization of computers have changed the whole *technology* of quantitative research and psychological testing. Factor analyses, item analyses, regression equations and the like can be turned out more easily and rapidly than simple correlations once were. One new conceptual development on the horizon may eventually make considerable difference in the way we design tests. Computers now make it feasible to *individualize* testing — to select for each person an optimum set of items in order to maximize the accuracy with which his or her potential and attainment are evaluated. The time is yet to come, however, when such testing constitutes standard practice.

The most clear difference between 1970 and 1978 is in public attitude toward psychological measurement. At present writing this appears to be considerably less favorable than it was in 1970. Doubts have been expressed about the social utility of the whole testing enterprise. Some are concerned about possible biases in aptitude tests that may tend to exclude the poor and the uneducated from opportunities to improve their condition. Others fear that the kinds of questions asked in personality inventories violate the individual's right to privacy. Still others are worried about the consequences of data banks in which individuals' test scores become permanent parts of their records, retrievable years later, possibly to their disadvantage.

These are valid concerns. We have attempted to deal with them in the appropriate sections of this revision, to make sure that the general consumer of test information for whom the book is written does not overlook them.

In general, we hope that this revision will continue to assist the consumer of test information and, furthermore, contribute to a more intelligent understanding and use of psychological tests.

We wish to express our appreciation to the following reviewers of this revision: Ric Brown, California State University at Fresno; David Goldstein, Temple University; Thelma Hunt, George Washington University; Jimmy L. Smith, Chattanooga State Technical Community College; Glen E. Thomas, Brigham Young University.

LEONA E. TYLER
W. BRUCE WALSH

The Nature
and Function
of Measurement
in Psychology

People need to understand their own natures. It has been reiterated to the point of triteness that the major problems our world faces today are human problems, and that the main stumbling blocks in the way of progress are human obstacles. Furthermore, now that society has evolved into a highly complex system of specialized roles and relationships, it needs new tools that will help individuals to find suitable places for themselves within the over-all structure.

It is these urgent needs of our time that make it necessary for psychology to become a science. The literary and philosophical descriptions of human nature that constituted psychology in past eras are being superseded in our time by accounts based on empirical research. In order to conduct the kind of research psychologists wished to do, they undertook to *quantify* the variables with which they worked, and thus measurement became a prominent feature of modern psychology.

To many students this is an unwelcome fact. They come to psychology to increase their understanding of the reasons why they and the people they know feel and act as they do, only to find themselves confronted with concepts that appear very remote from human concerns—standard deviations, frequency distributions, probabilities. It is little wonder that they rebel against and complain about the requirements set up for the psychology courses they elect. They question the relevance of mathematical concepts and quantitative formulations for a person whose objective is to obtain a working knowledge of psychology.

1

But the fact is that quantitative thinking is an essential rather than a peripheral feature of psychology today. The progress made during the last century would, indeed, have been impossible without it. In the first place, quantitative methods permit us to draw precise conclusions from experiments. In conducting an experiment, what we do is to apply some special procedure to animal or human subjects and note its effects. But it is apparent to any careful observer that reactions to stimulating situations *vary* a great deal from person to person. At a sudden clap of thunder, for instance, one person rushes to the window to catch sight of the lightning flashes, another turns away. So, too, in experiments, reactions vary greatly. Without some way of answering the questions "How much?" and "How many?" the outcomes of almost all experiments involving more than one subject thus become contradictory and confused. And unless we study more than one subject, we cannot expect to find out much about human nature.

In studying the learning process, for example, a psychologist may wish to find out whether it is better to present assignments in elementary logic in a way that prevents students from making errors or in one that permits them to make errors and then correct them. (Such questions become important when we undertake the practical task of constructing programs for computer-assisted instruction.) In setting up an experiment to answer this question, the psychologist would work out ways of quantifying the performance of his or her subjects in as many aspects as possible. Anticipating that they will not all react in the same way to the experimental conditions, the psychologist will not be surprised if some persons score higher under Condition A, some score higher under Condition B, and some do equally well under both. And it may turn out that Method A enables some subjects to learn very rapidly, but at the cost of not retaining what they learn, whereas Method B may take longer but facilitate retention. Clearly, the psychologist must have many complex possibilities in mind while planning the experiment.

So different kinds of measurements would be required to evaluate these possibilities. Thus, we might measure first the time each subject requires to reach a certain level of performance, or give a test of logical thinking immediately after the experimental procedure, and again a month later. We might devise tests for other kinds of mental ability thought to be related to logical reasoning, such as practical problem-solving or the detection of errors in propaganda. For each set of scores, we would compare the averages for Groups A and B, making use of statistical methods that would permit us to come to a conclusion stated in terms of probabilities. What we report, then, would take this form: "In our sample Method B came out better, and there are less than five chances in a hundred that a difference of this size could have arisen in a sample from a population in which no true difference existed." Without quantifying our data we could have drawn no conclusions at all; with quantification we can make a statement of *probability* upon which to base further decisions—either to proceed with one of the methods or to do another experiment.

Thus, measurements help psychologists make decisions about what their research means. Measurements also facilitate decisions about individuals. Psychologists began their efforts to construct mental tests because tools that would help make such decisions were needed. The ancestor of our present-day intelligence tests was Alfred Binet's 1905 scale. Binet developed this test as a means for helping Parisian school authorities decide which children were really unable to profit by the regular school program, no matter how they tried. Whatever can be said about the misuses of intelligence tests from Binet's time to our own—and there are many serious and valid criticisms that can be made—they have in countless instances enabled teachers to distinguish between the dull and the lazy far more efficiently than they could otherwise have done.

Let's take another example. During the 1930s, the public employment services throughout this country faced what looked like an impossible task. Thousands of people had lost their jobs because of the depression, and thousands of boys and girls were coming out of school each year seeking work. One major difficulty, of course, was that there were just not enough jobs to go around. But another, almost as serious, was that a large proportion of the job seekers, if they were to be placed at all, had to find new lines of work, jobs in which they had had no previous experience. This situation led to the initiation of a large-scale program to develop vocational aptitude tests designed to help predict how successful a person would be at an occupation *before* entering it. What grew out of this effort was the two and one-half hour General Aptitude Test Battery (GATB) which made it possible to evaluate an individual's suitability for hundreds of different jobs.

Another kind of decision in which psychologists participated fostered a whole new family of tests and measurement techniques. As more and more people have become interested in mental health and aware that psychological ills can be treated, demand for *personality tests* has grown. When a patient comes to a mental hospital or clinic, it is helpful to determine at the outset what kind of person this individual is and how he or she is likely to respond to treatment. Take the case of, say, Lawrence Gibbs. Should his condition be labeled "schizophrenia" or "anxiety reaction"? His psychiatrist may be looking for clues about whether Gibbs will respond better to hospital treatment or to therapy at a clinic in his own community. And if he enters the hospital, should he be assigned to a therapy group, or would some form of individual treatment carry a better prognosis? These are complex decisions that can seldom be made with any great certainty, but personality tests of several kinds can help in making them.

Measurement techniques are also important in situations where individuals must make decisions about their own lives. In some ways, these decisions *by* a person are more complex than decisions *about* a person. Many of the factors entering into them cannot usually be quantified—highly personal factors such as Henry's knowledge that his mother will be terribly disappointed if he does not go into the ministry, or Mr. Merton's feeling about a job that requires him to be away from home for long periods of time. But the fact that there are quantitative answers to some questions often simplifies such situations enough to make satisfactory decisions obtainable. The score on one kind of test, for example, will tell a college senior who is trying to decide whether to go on to graduate school or to go into business how he or she compares in complex intellectual abilities with successful graduate students in the major area. The score on another kind of test will enable the individual to judge how similar his or her interests are to those of both business people and scholars in the field. Day after day, in high school and college counseling offices, psychological measurements contribute to such decisions.

Thus, testing techniques and the statistical methods that go with them have been woven into the whole fabric of general and applied psychology. We shall now examine in more detail the ideas and the tools that are used. Real skill in the use of these methods requires a long apprenticeship, but a general understanding of the basic principles is within the reach of everyone—as parent, teacher, businessperson, or just plain citizen.

LEVELS OF MEASUREMENT

Measurement, as psychologists use the term, covers a wide range of activities. The only thing they all have in common is the use of numbers. The most general definition of measurement we can formulate is simply that measurement means the assignment of numerals according to rules.

These *rules* are not always as restrictive as persons with limited mathematical knowledge often think they are. Unless we have given the matter a good deal of thought, we are likely to assume that all the operations of elementary arithmetic—addition, subtraction, multiplication, and division—ought to be applicable to all measuring systems. Thus, our first reaction may be to conclude that measurement is impossible unless some arithmetical operation can obviously be applied. Take the whole field of intelligence testing, for example. Ever since these tests first came into use, thoughtful persons have pointed out that it really makes no sense to say that an individual with an IQ of 150 is twice as bright as one with an IQ of 75. That the two are very different in their responses to situations calling for abstract reasoning is true, but there is no justification to be found anywhere in their behavior for expressing this difference as a quotient of two, a fraction of one-half, or a ratio of two to one. It is just not meaningful to *divide* one IQ by another.

Once psychologists became aware of this peculiarity in some of the numbers they were using, they realized that there were parallel situations outside psychology. Take temperature, for example, as we ordinarily measure it on our Fahrenheit or Centigrade scales. If the temperature drops from 80° F during the day to 40° F during the night, we do not say that it was half as warm at midnight as it was at noon. Because zero in the Fahrenheit system is an arbitrary figure that does not really mean "no warmth at all," the number of degrees above zero cannot be handled in the same way that a measurement of height or weight can. Clearly, measurements of intelligence are more like those of temperature than those of height.

The general formulation of different kinds, or levels, of measurement that has been most useful to psychologists is the one set up by S. S. Stevens (1951). According to this system, we can divide the possible ways of assigning numerals into four types. Each of these varieties of measurement has rules and restrictions of its own. And, for each, certain statistical procedures are appropriate.

The Stevens system, as shown in Figure 1, arranges these levels of measurement according to the extent familiar arithmetical procedures are applicable. The first, or lowest, in the series is the *nominal* scale. Where this kind of scale applies, numbers are assigned only to identify the *categories* to which individual persons or things belong. These can be one-of-a-kind classifications, like placing numbers on football jerseys to identify the players. Or they can be labels that apply to *groups* of persons, as when men are given a code number of 1, women a code number of 2. The only arithmetical operation applicable to nominal scales is counting, the mere enumeration of individuals in each class. The identifying numerals themselves can never be added, subtracted, multiplied, or divided.

The next level of measurement is the *ordinal* scale. We use this when we are able to arrange individuals in a series ranging from lowest to highest according to the characteristic we wish to measure, but cannot say exactly how much difference there is between any two of them. When a committee ranks five scholarship candidates for over-all merit, it is using an ordinal scale. The percentile scores often used in reporting test results to students, since they too are a kind of ranking, also constitute ordinal measurement. The common arithmetical operations—addition, subtraction, multiplication, and division—cannot be legitimately used with ordinal scales, but statistical procedures based on ranks are appropriate. It is possible, for example, to determine whether the ranks of a group of children on popularity are related to their ranks on dependability.

The third level of measurement is the *interval* scale. What distinguishes interval from ordinal measurement is that it permits us to state just how far apart two things or persons are. Most school tests are of this type. Although there is some question about their measurement properties, teachers usually regard the scores on course examinations as interval scales. They consider it legitimate to compare the scores of two students and to tell Jerry that his score is 16 points lower than Bill's. But interval scales do have one important limitation. They have no real zero point. It is true that a student may occasionally come out with a *score* of zero on a test of trigonometry or English literature. But this does not mean that the student has no knowledge whatever of the subject. Although the purpose of the test is to measure knowledge of subject matter, it is not really necessary to define what "zero knowledge" means in order to do so, since we will be using the test mainly to compare individuals with one another.

Though we may add and subtract scores on interval scales, one arithmetical operation is never legitimate—that is, to *divide* one score by another, since division presupposes the existence of an exact zero point. Why not? Consider for a moment an examination in which Louise scores 80 and Marie 40. Now suppose that in writing this examination, the instructor had happened to include ten other questions easy enough for both girls to answer correctly. In this case Louise would have scored 90, Marie 50. The difference between their scores would be 40 points in either case, but the quotient of the two scores would not be the same. Instead of 2 (80 ÷ 40), it would be 1.8 (90 ÷ 50). With any particular test, then, we have no way of finding out whether one person's knowledge is twice as great, three times as great, or one-and-a-half times as great as that of another person. But

LEVEL	LIMITATIONS	ILLUSTRATION
IV — RATIO SCALES Each number can be thought of as a distance measured from zero.	There are no limitations. All arithmetical operations and all statistical techniques are permissible.	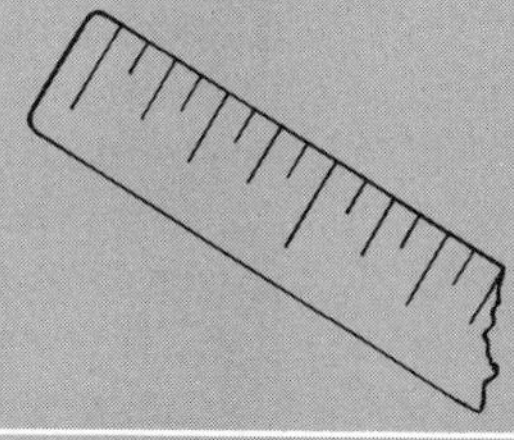
III — INTERVAL SCALES The intervals or distances between each number and the next are equal, but it is not known how far any of them is from zero.	In addition to procedures listed below, addition and subtraction and statistical techniques based on these arithmetical operations are permissible. Multiplication and division are not permissible.	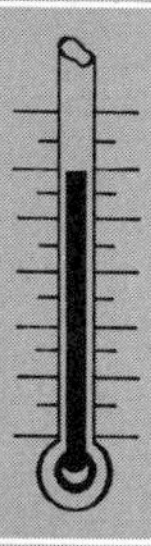
II — ORDINAL SCALES Numbers indicate rank or order.	In addition to procedures below, ranking methods and other statistical techniques based on interpretations of "greater than" or "less than" are permissible.	
I — NOMINAL SCALES Numbers are used to name, identify, or classify.	The only permissible arithmetical procedures are counting and the statistical techniques based on counting.	

Figure 1. The Levels of Measurement.

if we can assume that each question is an equally good indicator of knowledge of the field, we do not violate any principles of mathematics or logic when we subtract one score from another or when we add a number of scores together and take an average. The statistical methods used to translate raw scores on tests into various kinds of derived scores—methods we shall be considering in a later chapter—rest on addition and subtraction exclusively.

The fourth and highest level of measurement is the *ratio scale.* With it all arithmetical operations can be used—addition, subtraction, multiplication, and division. Ratio scales have all the characteristics of interval scales, with the additional advantage of a true zero point. We are probably more familiar with such scales than with any of the other types because all common physical dimensions— height, weight, volume—can be measured this way. On the scales of an honest butcher, zero means that no meat at all has been placed on the pan, and when we buy the meat we can confidently say that a six-pound roast is four pounds heavier than a two-pound roast; it also makes sense to say that it is *three times* as heavy. The name *ratio scale* signifies that we can divide one number by another or express the two as a ratio.

Many of the measurements we make in psychology fail to qualify as ratio scales, but a few of them do. These few usually occur where it is possible to measure a mental characteristic in physical units of some sort. When we measure reaction time, for example, we use the customary time units, seconds and fractions of a second. If we are interested in determining how quickly would-be automobile drivers can step on a brake pedal in response to a red light, we can do so with a ratio scale. Thus, if it takes John five-tenths of a second and Bill only three-tenths of a second, we can, if we like, make a 3:5 ratio of these two scores to describe how much quicker Bill is than John. Still, even when we are working with a ratio scale, as in this instance, we may not wish to make ratios or divide one number by another. For all the methods permissible at lower levels of measurement can be used at a higher one. In practical applications of studies of reaction time, for instance, what the investigator would probably want to know about both John and Bill is how they compare with norms, or standards, for adequate drivers. Such comparisons involve only subtraction, not ratio-making.

In the years since Stevens put forward this system for classifying levels of measurement, there has been a vast amount of discussion about what are and what are not legitimate ways of handling particular kinds of psychological data. Unfortunately, not all sets of numbers fall as clearly into one or another of the four classes as do the illustrations used in Figure 1. Telephone numbers, for example, are probably nominal, for identification only. But how about Zip Codes? The first digits alone constitute some sort of ordinal scale signifying how far west the designated area is. What kinds of numerical operation can we apply to Zip Codes?

Deciding whether a set of measurements falls in the ordinal or the interval category is also sometimes troublesome. Dr. X, for example, comes out with a conclusion that anxiety and creativity are linked together to some degree, supporting the statement with evidence that in the group of high school students tested there was a correlation of .36 between measures of the two characteristics. Dr. Y objects to Dr. X's conclusion on the grounds that there is no assurance that anxiety and creativity were measured on interval scales, and thus it was not legitimate to correlate the scores in the way Dr. X did.

One of the means developed for avoiding disputes of this sort is to consider the mathematical systems that are applied to data to be *models,* analogous to the models geologists construct in order to study the characteristics of river systems or mountain ranges. If the observations based on the model that has been set up lead to conclusions that do not work out in practice or in further research, the model can be abandoned and a better one substituted. Since it is advantageous statistically to work with interval scales whenever possible (it is clear at the outset that most psychological measurements do not have fixed zero points and thus cannot be considered ratio scales), one usually begins by assuming that a new measuring device will produce an interval scale. If the investigation leads to conclusions that do not seem reasonable, one can reanalyze the results with statistical techniques based on an assumption that only an ordinal scale is present. In the example given in the previous paragraph, the correlation of anxiety and creativity would probably be a little higher on an interval scale than on an ordinal scale, but the conclusion about the extent and significance of the relationship is likely to be the same in either case. Thinking in terms of abstract models, mathematical and other varieties, has freed psychologists of the necessity of making unprovable statements about the nature of their data.

It has also become increasingly clear that, like etiquette and language usage, our systems of measurement are to a considerable extent based on *convention.* As long as researchers follow the same conventions, they understand one another. As increasing amounts of evidence accumulate, some of the conventions are changed, just as football rules are modified from year to year by the associations that have jurisdiction over them.

For the consumer, in contrast to the producer, of psychological measurements, the most important caution to be observed is to remember that not all of the operations we know how to carry out with numbers can legitimately be used with test scores and other numerical evaluations of psychological characteristics. The IQ we find recorded in a student's school record is a *different kind of number* from the measurement of height or weight that precedes it. And percentile scores entered in the same record for reading and arithmetic tests the student has taken constitute a different kind of number from either the IQ or the physical measurements.

With this fundamental understanding that numbers may not always mean what we think they mean, let us turn to some of the statistical ideas we must grasp if we are to use psychological measurements intelligently.

Basic
Statistics

2

ORDER IN VARIATION

At the beginning of the previous chapter, we raised the problem of variation from person to person. More than a century ago, Lambert A. Quetelet, a Belgian mathematician, discovered a kind of order in individual variations that impressed him deeply. Quetelet worked mainly with census data and measures of physical characteristics, but it was not long before Sir Francis Galton, the brilliant English scientist, was applying Quetelet's methods, and others he himself developed, to measurement of characteristics like "acuteness of vision"—traits we would now classify as psychological.

The method these early workers hit upon—one that has been in constant use ever since—was to obtain measurements on a large group of individuals, and then arrange the results in order from lowest to highest in what they called a frequency distribution. In these distributions they found the same pattern showing up again and again, a pattern that can be illustrated by Galton's measurements of the chest girths of more than 5000 soldiers, shown in Figure 2.

The pattern, when a distribution is pictured in a graph, is a bell-shaped curve. A large number of cases clusters near the middle of the distribution, forming the average, or central tendency. The farther from this average a measurement lies, the smaller the proportion of the total group to whom it applies. Thus, there are many chest measurements of 39, 40, and 41 inches, but only a few as low as 33 or as high as 48. Quetelet, Galton, and other nineteenth-

11

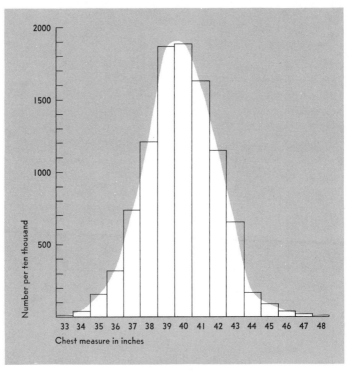

Figure 2. Chest measurements of 5738 soldiers. *(From F. Galton.* Hereditary Genius: An Inquiry into Its Laws, *Appleton, 1870; reprinted in New York: Horizon Press, 1952. Chapter 3.)*

century workers found such a beautiful regularity in the distributions of trait after trait that they came to believe there was some universal law governing human differences.

This symmetrical, bell-shaped curve was already familiar to mathematicians. They had discovered it as they studied the outcomes of games of chance—coin-tossing, dice-throwing, and the like—and had worked out the mathematical equation for the curve of the distribution obtained with an infinitely large number of events, each determined by what we call "chance." This *normal probability* curve (or *Gaussian* curve, as it is called in honor of the mathematician who formulated its equation) became one of the foundations of modern statistics. To Quetelet and Galton, this equation seemed to apply equally well to the distributions of measurements they had collected. The word "normal," as used in statistics, applies to this curve and carries no connotation of "right" or "best."

As time has passed, it has become clear that human measurements, especially measurements of psychological traits, do not always yield a Gaussian distribution. Some distributions are *skewed*, meaning that there are either too many high scores or too many low scores in the group to produce the symmetry of the normal distribution curve; others are too *peaked* or *stretched out* to fit the normal curve equation. These require special equations. But since statistical methods based on normal distributions are easier to use and interpret than those based on less common mathematical formulations, test makers often make a special effort to collect items that will result in a normal distribution in the group for which a test is intended. Thus, if the group on which preliminary norms are based turns out to have too many low scores, it is possible to take out some of the harder test questions and replace them with easier ones. If there is not enough spread, items can be added that will produce more low and high scores. For some testing purposes, nonnormal distributions are deliberately sought. In short, methods for analyzing the characteristics of each question in a test now make it possible to select items in a manner that will produce any desired distribution. The majority of well-standardized tests yield normal distributions when large groups are tested.

In Figure 3 we see such a distribution for a test that was for years the leading measure of children's intelligence. While there are

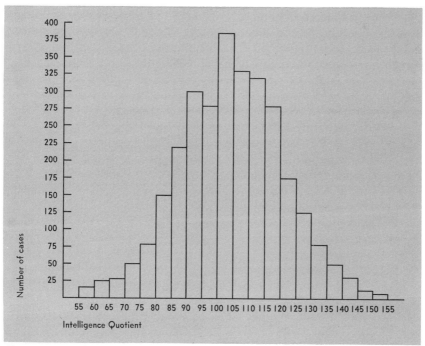

Figure 3. Distribution of IQ's on form L of the Stanford-Binet test for ages 2½ to 18. *(From Q. McNemar. The Revision of the Stanford-Binet Scale. Boston: Houghton Mifflin Company, 1942.)*

a few minor irregularities, they are not great enough to constitute a serious departure from the normal form. There are large numbers of IQ's in the neighborhood of 100, very few near the extremes of 55 and 155. (A very small proportion of the population scores lower and higher than the arbitrary end points shown here.)

MEASURES OF CENTRAL TENDENCY

In summarizing a distribution of measurements for a group, we must always report two characteristics. First, we must describe in some way the *central tendency*, most commonly by computing what we ordinarily call an average, but what statisticians call the *arithmetic mean*. To get this figure, we simply add all the scores together and divide by the number of cases. There are two other kinds of averages, however, that are preferable for some distributions—the median and the mode. The *median* is simply the *middle* score in a distribution, or the number that would represent a point between the two middle ones. The *mode* is the *most common* score, the one made by the most persons. In Table 1 we see what the mean, median, and mode would be for one set of figures. We can also see why we might prefer one to the others. Parents who wished to pay their child for allowance an amount that conformed to the central tendency of the group might well be dissatisfied with the arithmetic mean as an average here. This is why: The two boys in the group who receive

Table 1

Central Tendency Determinations for a Distribution of Weekly Allowances Received by 20 Boys in a School Class

BOY	ALLOWANCE	BOY	ALLOWANCE
1	$.10	11	$ .25
2	.10	12	.25
3	.10	13	.25
4	.15	14	.25
5	.15	15	.25
6	.15	16	.30
7	.20	17	.30
8	.20	18	.35
9	.20	19	1.00
10	.20	20	1.00

Mean   = $5.75 ÷ 20 = $0.2875, or $0.29
Median = Between $0.20 and $0.25, or $0.23
Mode   = $0.25

$1.00 allowances are not at all typical. Adding these figures in with the others inflates the total so that the mean, 29¢, is too high to be really characteristic of the group as a whole. The median of 22½¢ seems fairer in this case. But the most convenient index of central tendency here is the mode of 25¢, the amount received by the greatest number of boys.

In a distribution that is exactly normal, the mean, median, and mode are identical, so it makes no difference which one we use as a measure of central tendency. Since few distributions turn out to be *exactly* normal, however, we must usually decide which is the most convenient and meaningful. Often the choice depends on what other uses we plan to make of the scores besides just citing an average.

MEASURES OF VARIABILITY

The second kind of index we need in order to describe a distribution of scores is some measure of *variability*. How much of a *spread* is there in the distribution? It obviously makes a difference to a school-teacher, for example, whether the range of reading scores in the class is from 50 to 150 or from 90 to 110. In both classes, the average score is about 100, but the first group would require much more diversification of reading materials than the second one would. The simplest way to describe this variability is to subtract the lowest score from the highest one. This gives us the index called the *range*. In the example just given, the range in the first classroom is 100 points, in the second 20 points.

The disadvantage of the range is that a single high or low score tends to carry too much weight. In a group of 1000 school children, for example, there may be only one who receives a score of 100 on an arithmetic test. The next highest person scores 82. To say that scores range from zero to 100 is a little misleading and gives the wrong impression about how variable the group actually is. A far more satisfactory index of variability in a group, one that does not unduly emphasize extreme cases, is the *standard deviation*. The formula is SD

$$\sqrt{\frac{\Sigma d^2}{N}}$$

(where d stands for "deviation from the mean," N, of course, stands for the number of persons in the group, and the Greek symbol Σ stands for "sum," thus instructing the reader to *add* the numbers to which it applies, in this case all squared deviations). Table 2 shows

Table 2

Computation of the Standard Deviation for a Distribution of
the Scores Made by Eleven Children on a Spelling Test

CHILD	SCORE	DEVIATION FROM MEAN	SQUARED DEVIATIONS
Elaine	20	+6	36
Martha	18	+4	16
Bill	15	+1	1
Jim	15	+1	1
Edna	14	0	0
Harry	14	0	0
Marie	14	0	0
Joe	13	−1	1
Lucy	13	−1	1
John	10	−4	16
Grant	8	−6	36
	154		108

Mean = 154 ÷ 11 = 14
Variance = 108 ÷ 11 = 9.82
Standard deviation = $\sqrt{9.82}$ = 3.1

how it is computed. First we obtain the mean, or average, score in the customary way. Then we subtract this figure from each of the individual scores. Next we square each of these deviations. To find out what the *average* of these squared deviations is, we divide their total by the number of cases, which gives us what statisticians call the *variance* of the distribution. To obtain the *standard deviation* we take the square root of the variance.

It is readily apparent that the standard deviation does not have the defect we noted in the range—its magnitude does not depend greatly on single extreme scores. On the contrary, each score in the distribution contributes to the standard deviation. In distributions where scores cluster quite closely around the mean, the standard deviation will naturally be small. In distributions where scores spread out a good deal on both sides of the mean, the standard deviation will be large.

Where the distribution of scores is normal, a person who knows the mean and standard deviation does not need to *see* the whole distribution in order to grasp its major characteristics. The use of means and standard deviations thus furnishes us with a valuable shorthand way of comparing groups and individuals within groups. We will explain in more detail in a later section (p. 41) how we make such comparisons.

MEASURES OF RELATIONSHIP

Besides measures of central tendency and variability, one other statistical device is indispensable in dealing with measurements of human traits. When, as is often the case, we must *relate* one set of scores to another, we use the *correlation coefficient*. Although there are many ways of computing correlations, one technique, which yields an index called the *product-moment coefficient*, is the most common.

It is also possible—and helpful—to indicate graphically, by a scatter diagram, the extent to which two measures are related. So before we delve into the computation of the product-moment coefficient, let us look first at Figure 4, a scatter diagram that plots the correlation between the spelling scores of the eleven children in Table 2 and their arithmetic scores. On this graph one mark indicates each child's scores in both subjects. Martha's scores, for example, are on the line extending upward from a spelling score of 18 and on the line extending to the right from an arithmetic score of 25. In a diagram of this sort, we can judge how closely related two measure-

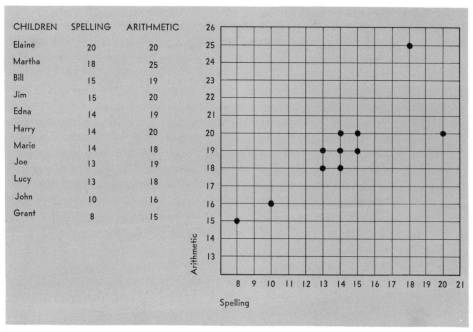

CHILDREN	SPELLING	ARITHMETIC
Elaine	20	20
Martha	18	25
Bill	15	19
Jim	15	20
Edna	14	19
Harry	14	20
Marie	14	18
Joe	13	19
Lucy	13	18
John	10	16
Grant	8	15

Figure 4. Scatter diagram showing relationship between spelling and arithmetic scores made by eleven children.

ments are by seeing how closely the entries lie to a single line that might be drawn from the lower left to the upper right corner. If all entries are on such a line, the relationship between the two scores portrayed is perfect. In this case, it would mean that each child was exactly as much above or below the group average in arithmetic as he or she was in spelling. This is not quite the case, however, for the scores in Figure 4. There is a strong general trend for scores to fall *near* such a diagonal line, but they are not exactly *on it*. A scatter diagram gives a vivid but rough picture of such a relationship. We often need to refine our understanding.

The product-moment correlation coefficient (r) is a precise mathematical statement of the relationship between two such sets of scores. Its formula is:

$$r = \frac{\Sigma(d_x)\,(d_y)}{N(SD_x)\,(SD_y)}$$

(In this formula the letter d, again, stands for deviation from the mean, N stands for the number of cases, SD_x stands for the standard deviation of the first set of scores, and SD_y stands for the standard deviation of the second set of scores). Table 3 shows how we compute it. First we find the mean and standard deviation for each set of scores. (These are computed for spelling scores in Table 2; the same procedure is followed for the arithmetic scores.) We then multiply each person's deviation from the group mean for spelling by the deviation from the group mean for arithmetic. The algebraic sum of these deviation *products* forms the numerator of the fraction in the equation. We then proceed to obtain the denominator in the fraction by multiplying the number of cases by the product of the two standard deviations.

If the relationship between two variables is perfect, r will be 1.00. For all lesser degrees of relationship, it will turn out to be a decimal number less than 1.00. In our example, r = .83. We can understand why this is as high as it is, and also why it is not 1.00, if we examine the deviations. The children who are above average on the spelling test are also above average on the arithmetic test, except for Bill. The children who are below average in spelling are also below average in arithmetic, except for Joe. Elaine is a little higher in spelling than Martha is, while Martha is higher than Elaine in arithmetic. But generally speaking, each of these children is just about as successful in arithmetic as in spelling. It is precisely such relationships that a high correlation (here .83) indicates. Just as the mean and standard deviation are shorthand descriptions of one dis-

Table 3

Computation of the Product-Moment Correlation Coefficient for Scores Made by Eleven Children on Spelling and Arithmetic Tests

CHILD	SPELLING	ARITHMETIC	SPELLING DEVIATION FROM MEAN	ARITHMETIC DEVIATION FROM MEAN	PRODUCT OF DEVIATIONS
Elaine	20	20	+6	+1	+6
Martha	18	25	+4	+6	+24
Bill	15	19	+1	0	0
Jim	15	20	+1	+1	+1
Edna	14	19	0	0	0
Harry	14	20	0	+1	0
Marie	14	18	0	−1	0
Joe	13	19	−1	0	0
Lucy	13	18	−1	−1	+1
John	10	16	−4	−3	+12
Grant	8	15	−6	−4	+24
	154	209			+68

Spelling mean = 154 ÷ 11 = 14
Arithmetic mean = 209 ÷ 11 = 19
Spelling standard deviation (computed in Table 2) = 3.1
Arithmetic standard deviation (computed in manner shown in Table 2) = 2.4

$$\text{Product-moment correlation } (r) = \frac{68}{(11) \times (3.1) \times (2.4)}$$
$$r = .83$$

tribution, so a correlation coefficient provides a summary of the relationship between two.

Many of the correlations the psychologist runs into are lower than the one we have been considering, and sometimes they are negative. A negative correlation in our example would have told us that low scores in spelling tend to go with high scores in arithmetic; and vice versa. Had the correlation turned out to be about zero, it would have told us that there is *no* relationship, in other words, that the whole range of combinations of low and high scores in arithmetic and spelling occur equally often. A moderate correlation, such as .50, would reveal that individuals tend to score about as high in one trait as they do on the other, but that there are numerous exceptions to this general trend.

Correlation techniques have been indispensable in the development of usable mental tests. Had we not been able to analyze what characteristics are *related* to one another, we should never have been able to find out what a new test measures or how accurately it measures anything at all. Just how correlations are used for these purposes will be considered in the next chapter, which is on tests.

STATISTICAL SIGNIFICANCE AND CHANCE

So far we have been looking at statistical methods designed to *describe* distributions compactly. But statistics also provides convenient techniques for making *inferences* about *other* persons and events that are not part of a group originally studied. The methods used for this purpose are sometimes complex and difficult to grasp, but anyone who works with psychological measurements should understand the basic reasoning behind them.

The fundamental idea is that any one group of persons or things we choose to measure constitutes a *sample* of a larger population. When we carry on research, it is that general population about which we really wish to draw conclusions rather than the particular sample we happen to test. Thus, the eleven children whose spelling and arithmetic scores we have been examining are only a small part of a numerous group of children their age. Whether the population of 10-year-olds we are interested in is in one town, one state, one country, or the whole world, the principle is the same: These children constitute a sample; we would like to infer from their scores something about spelling and arithmetic performance in the population.

The problem of how samples are related to populations has been studied through both practical procedures and mathematical reasoning. In the practical, empirical kind of study, an investigator may shake dice again and again, work out the mean of each 10 throws, and analyze the differences among these "chance" samples of 10 from a "population" that consists of, say, 10,000 throws. Mathematical reasoning accomplishes the same purpose with less effort. What we find in both cases is that the drawing of repeated samples from the same population produces a *distribution* of whatever statistic we are computing—a normal one if the population from which the samples are drawn has a normal distribution. The mean and standard deviation of this *sampling distribution* can be estimated from the information we have about a few samples, or even one sample alone. In Figure 5 we see what the sampling distribution of means for samples of 25 would be for a population with a mean of 100 and a standard deviation of 20. We need not go into the mathematical relationships or the formulas used to make the computations. The only important fact to be gleaned from Figure 5 is that the variability of the *means* of samples of 25 is *much smaller* than the variability of scores in the population from which samples are drawn.

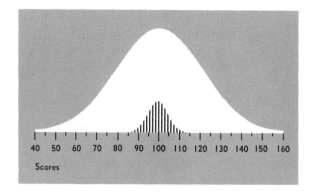

Figure 5. Hypothetical normal distribution of scores for an infinitely large population in which the mean is 100 and the standard deviation is 20. Also the hypothetical distribution of means that would be obtained if many samples of 25 were drawn at random from such a population.

There is a special name for the standard deviation of the sampling distribution, a standard deviation that indicates how much variability there is in a *statistic* rather than in people or events. It is *standard error*. Since we can compute any statistic we like in samples and in populations, there are many kinds of standard error—standard error of a mean, standard error of a difference between two means, standard error of a correlation coefficient, standard error of a score. For whichever kind, the standard error is a way of showing us what degree of variation, with regard to the statistical unit in question, we can expect in different samples of the same population.

The concept of sampling distributions enables us to estimate the probability that any result we have obtained could have occurred by "chance." Chance is simply a label for whatever unknown factors there are that cause samples to differ. Why does one throw of the dice turn up different numbers from another? Chance. Why do answers on a public opinion poll vary a little from group to group, even when respondents are chosen in exactly the same way? Chance.

To illustrate this reasoning, let us compare some scores to find out whether the difference between two means is a matter of chance. Suppose that the teacher of our eleven children adopts a new method to make them better spellers. After a month of intensive training under the new method, the children take a second test known to be exactly equal in difficulty to the first one. Their scores on the first and second tests are shown in Table 4. It is clear that the average for the class had gone up from 14 to 16. While there was one child who actually scored lower on the second test than she did on the first, all of the rest improved to varying extents. But is this 2-point difference really so large that it could not have occurred by chance if we had taken a second sample of these children's spelling without giving them any special teaching at all? It is this sort of question that the t statistic was designed to answer. What t is, is the ratio of difference between means to the standard error of the difference. (There is, of course, one other possibility—that the 2-point difference represents not chance variation but a gain resulting from what was learned by taking the first test. To allow for this would require a more complicated research design. For the time being, we will ignore the possibility.) Before considering what t means, let us see how it is computed.

First of all, we determine the difference between the two scores for each individual in the group. Then we work out the mean and standard deviation of this distribution of *differences* just as we do for single scores. (In one respect this computation differs from the one shown in Table 2. In inferential, unlike descriptive, statistics, for reasons it is not necessary to go into here, we divide the total of the squared deviations by one less than the total number of individuals in the group, in this case by 10 rather than 11.) To get the standard error of the difference between two means (the standard deviation of the sampling distribution for such differences), we divide the standard deviation of the differences by the square root of the total number of cases. (Again, we need not go into the mathematical reasons for this procedure.) The t ratio consists of the mean of the differences divided by the standard error of the differences. In this case, it turns out to be 3.3. From tables of t, available in all standard statistics texts, we learn that this is statistically significant at the .01 level (represented as $P < .01$ in Table 4).

This last phrase, translated into the language of samples and populations and applied to our example, means that no more than once in a hundred times would a group of children like ours give us the results we obtained on the two tests if chance factors alone were operating. We can conclude with some confidence, then, that the special teaching method *was* effective.

It might not, of course, be effective for the reasons the teacher thinks it is. Other tryouts of the method under various conditions, as well as comparisons with groups taught in other ways, would probably be necessary before the teacher could be sure just why it worked.

There are many other versions of the t formula designed to be used with different kinds of data. But whatever technique is used, the outcome is a probability statement like the one in the example. These probability statements are what the term *statistical significance* refers to. A statistically significant difference is one that produces a t with a *small* probability. This means that it is *not* very likely that the difference in question would occur in chance samples in which the members had not been chosen in a special way or given special treatment. A statistically significant correlation is one

Table 4

Computation of the t Statistic to Test Whether an Increase in Spelling Scores Is Statistically Significant

CHILD	FIRST SCORE	SECOND SCORE	DIFFERENCE	DEVIATION FROM MEAN OF DIFFERENCE	SQUARED DEVIATION
Elaine	20	23	+3	+1	+1
Martha	18	20	+2	0	0
Bill	15	19	+4	+2	+4
Jim	15	15	0	−2	+4
Edna	14	11	−3	−5	+25
Harry	14	16	+2	0	0
Marie	14	18	+4	+2	+4
Joe	13	15	+2	0	0
Lucy	13	16	+3	+1	+1
John	10	13	+3	+1	+1
Grant	8	10	+2	0	0
	154	176	22		40

Mean of first test = 154 ÷ 11 = 14
Mean of second test = 176 ÷ 11 = 16
Mean of differences = 22 ÷ 11 = 2
Standard deviation of differences = $\sqrt{40/10}$ = $\sqrt{4.0}$ = 2.0
Standard error of difference = 2.0 ÷ $\sqrt{11}$
$\qquad\qquad$ = 2.0 ÷ 3.3 = .6

$$t = \frac{2 \text{ (Mean of difference)}}{.6 \text{ (Standard error of difference)}}$$
$\quad$ = 3.3
$P < .01$

that would have been unlikely to turn up, had we simply put down pairs of numbers at random and gone through the motions of computing r. The lower the probability value, then, the more certain we can be that our results represent something other than chance.

Anyone who reads research reports will repeatedly encounter such phrases as "significant at the .05 level." This is simply a way of stating what we have been talking about—of saying that results like those reported would have been expected by chance not more than five times out of a hundred. It is not customary to consider results that give probabilities larger than .05 to be "statistically significant," but the level varies somewhat in accordance with what the investigator is trying to find out.

Complicated and devious as this reasoning may seem to a novice, it represents only the most elementary level of inferential statistics. The question of whether a difference upon which one is basing some conclusion could have been obtained by chance is an important one. But there are other kinds of inferences research workers are frequently called upon to make. Sometimes they need to come up with as accurate an estimate as possible of what the mean or standard deviation of the population from which a given sample is drawn really is. Sometimes they need to decide whether a mathematical model they formulated to start with can be considered a satisfactory representation of the results actually obtained in a series of experiments. Sometimes they must estimate how many more persons should be asked to participate in an experiment in order to get a definitive answer to a particular research question. Working out special statistical techniques to solve these and many other kinds of problems has been a continuing challenge to mathematical statisticians. To be a scientist requires not only that one plan and conduct experiments, but also that one draw valid conclusions and only valid conclusions from the way these experiments turn out.

The development of statistical techniques that permit research workers to make inferences about whole populations from samples has enabled us to increase our knowledge far more rapidly than we could otherwise have done. Besides that, however, an understanding of these techniques, at least in a general way, is also useful to intelligent citizens who are not research workers, in that it helps them to evaluate what they hear and read about people and products, to draw some conclusion as to whether figures presented as evidence for the superiority of a new tooth paste, for example, really prove anything. Intricate as the reasoning included in statistical inferences is, mastering it is well worth the effort.

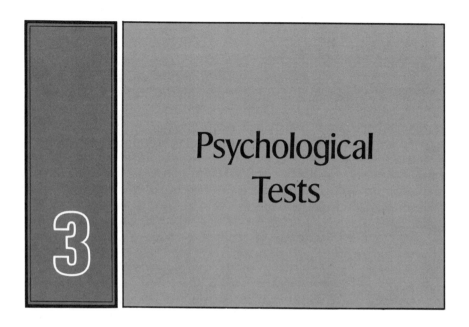

Psychological Tests

TESTS VERSUS MEASUREMENTS

So far we have not considered whether there is any distinction between the terms *test* and *measurement*. Although their meanings overlap, they are not quite synonyms. The latter word applies in many areas of psychological research where the former would not be appropriate. For example: Experimenters who study sensation, perception, and judgment make extensive use of *psychophysics*, that is, the measurement of physical magnitudes corresponding to psychological magnitudes (such things as how bright a light looks, or how loud a tone sounds). If the question under examination is, say, "What are the upper and lower limits of human hearing?" what they measure are vibration rates. The physical measurements are thus used to answer a psychological question.

It is customary to speak of a psychological measurement as a test when it is used primarily to assess some characteristic of an *individual* rather than to answer a general question like that about human hearing in the previous paragraph. Measurements of pitch thresholds can, of course, be used in this way as tests. But more typically a test consists of questions or tasks presented to the person who is to be examined, and the scores obtained are not expressed in physical units of any kind.

Thus, not all measurements are tests. But the reverse is also true—not all tests are measurements. There are some personality tests, for example, that do not produce scores. A psychologist may

25

use such a test to help formulate a verbal description of a person. Measurement, at any of the levels we distinguish in Chapter 1, need not be involved. In Chapter 1 *measurement* was defined as the assignment of numerals to things according to rules. A *test* can be defined as a standardized situation designed to elicit a sample of an individual's behavior. When that sample can be expressed as a numerical score, either *test* or *measurement* is an appropriate term.

Thus, even though the overlap between the concepts is not complete, we can still say that most tests are measuring techniques, and most psychological measurements can be used as tests. We shall take up in this chapter some ideas that apply particularly to tests.

HISTORICAL BACKGROUND

Throughout the years since psychology got started as a scientific enterprise (the date usually cited is the establishment of Wilhelm Wundt's laboratory in Leipzig in 1879), researchers have focused their efforts primarily on the search for general principles that would apply to everyone. Psychologists have tried to discover how the human eye and brain work together to produce the perceptions of color, shape, and size we all experience. They have set up experiments to study the learning process, expressing their findings as "laws of learning." They have studied human development, by comparing one age group with another, established norms of behavior for each age, and formulated theories about the developmental process.

All along, however, there has been a secondary focus of interest and effort. Even some of the earliest workers in the then-new German laboratories of experimental psychology turned their attention to the *variation* they encountered among subjects. These men, who often had a strong practical orientation, realized that measurements of differences among people might have important applications in schools, factories, and offices. An American who studied in Wundt's laboratory, James McKeen Cattell, was particularly influential in the movement to utilize psychological measurements as mental tests. It was he, in fact, who first used the term "mental test" in 1890, but there were others who figured prominently in the same movement during the closing years of the nineteenth century.

What these scientists were most eager to find was some quantitative way of assessing general intelligence. They thought they could obtain an index of intelligence if they could measure in combination in individuals all the characteristics that were being measured separately in the experimental laboratories—sensation, perception, attention, discrimination, speed of reaction, and so on. The superior individual, according to their reasoning, should be the one who ranks high in all these qualities. Though there is nothing obviously wrong with their reasoning, the attempt to measure intelligence in this way failed. For when the psychologists analyzed their measurements, they discovered that these traits were not closely correlated to one another. Furthermore, the sum of the scores did not appear to be an index of general intelligence. Poor students, for example, achieved just as high scores as good students did. Clearly, a different approach to the problem of measuring intelligence seemed to be required.

This new departure was soon made in France, when Alfred Binet started from the premise that intelligence is an inherently *complex* characteristic, not merely the sum of many simple traits. To measure it, he held, we must find ways of evaluating how individuals deal with tasks that require reasoning, judgment, and problem-solving. So over a period of years Binet tried out—on his own children and on children of different ages in the Paris schools— many kinds of tasks as potential tests of children's intelligence. At last in 1905, with the collaboration of Theophile Simon, he published the first real intelligence scale, the ancestor of all our present tests.

Progress was rapid from then on. The Binet-Simon scale was adapted for use in many countries. Tests suitable for adults were added to those designed especially for children. Group tests were produced during World War I and adapted soon afterward for use in schools and industries. Tests for many abilities not so broad and general as intelligence were constructed. Attempts to measure personality characteristics as well as abilities became more and more common. By the middle of the twentieth century, thousands of tests—good, bad, and indifferent—were in print.

In the course of all this activity on the mental-testing front, standards and principles emerged. In 1954 the American Psychological Association (APA) published the *Technical Recommendations for Psychological Tests and Diagnostic Techniques*. These recommendations were endorsed and extended by the American Educational Research Association (AERA) and the National Council on Measurement in Education in a document entitled *Technical Recommendations for Achievement Tests* (1955). In 1966 the three organizations in joint committee revised the two documents and published the *Standards for Educational and Psychological Tests and Manuals* (1966). The most recent revision (1974) was in the main stimulated by invasion-of-privacy problems and discrimination against minority groups. These *Standards for Educational and Psychological Tests* (1974), which concentrate on the test manual, serve as reasonable guides to those who wish to construct new tests and those who need to select wisely from the ones already available. For example, the standards indicate that a properly prepared manual reports the procedures followed in construction of the test (including reliability and validity data), in its use, and in the interpretation of the derived scores. In our test-conscious modern world, it has become virtually essential for an educated person to know something about these standards and principles. The teacher who wishes to adapt classroom instruction to the differing characteristics of the students, the parents who want to help their son or daughter make wise plans for education and career, the business person who hopes to avoid being duped by unscrupulous test publishers and sales people—all need a working knowledge of how tests are built and how they should be judged.

THE MEANING AND TYPES OF VALIDITY

The most important consideration is *validity*, which pertains to the question: "*What* does this test measure?" Unless we have a fairly adequate answer to this question, any test will be useless in our attempts to deal wisely with human beings—adults or children, ourselves or others. It may even be worse than useless, because if we act on the wrong assumption about what a person's score means, we may steer the individual toward decisions that will lead to maladjustment and costly mistakes.

Many persons fail to recognize that the title of a test really tells us nothing at all about what the test measures. Any individual can write a set of questions and be perfectly confident that they call for "reasoning" or "mechanical aptitude" or "cognitive flexibility" on the part of the respondent. But to find out what mental processes the testee must actually use to answer these questions is a long and arduous task. A test Mr. Smith constructs to measure "reasoning ability" may prove to be a test of middle-class attitudes. A "mechanical aptitude" test may turn out to measure mainly general intelligence. An "emotional maturity" inventory may measure only what testees know about the social desirability of certain behavior. The first knack one must acquire in evaluating the validity of tests is the habit of disregarding their titles. The important question is not

"What does the author *call* this test?" but "What are scores on this test *related to?*"

At the outset of the testing movement, the accepted procedure was to define first what one *intended* to measure and then collect evidence to show how successful one had been. During those years, as we saw, most efforts were directed toward the measurement of general intelligence. And although it became apparent as the number of investigators increased that they were not all defining this elusive term in exactly the same way, still, for practical purposes they were all assuming that intelligence is the trait on which judgments of brightness and dullness in school are based. Thus, they looked to school situations for evidence about the validity of intelligence tests. How close, they asked, is the relationship between the degree of school success predicted from test scores and the degree of success actually achieved? It was on the basis of the resulting evidence that the laboratory measurements of discrimination, reaction time, and the like, were discarded, and the Binet-type questions, calling for more complex responses, were retained in intelligence tests.

Such measurements of a psychological trait in a real-life situation, such as a schoolroom, are called *criterion* measurements. Correlations between test scores and criterion measurements are called *validity coefficients*.

To start with, then, validity meant *the extent to which a test measures what it purports to measure.* To find out how valid a test was, one was expected to correlate test scores with criterion measurements. But as time passed, it became clear that there were complications in both procedure and concept. Unfortunately, it is impossible in most instances to find any one criterion that will be an unambiguous indicator of a mental trait. Two psychologists investigating the same trait—mechanical aptitude, for example—may decide to use different criteria and so may achieve different results. Mr. Allen may think that the obvious measures to rely on are the grades high school boys receive in a shop course. Mr. Baker may think that the length of time it takes new men to learn a simple mechanical skill in a factory is the relevant criterion. Now, what if the test they both use correlates .06 with one of these criteria, .59 with the other? How are we to say how valid the test is when it gives results of this sort? Is it a test of mechanical aptitude or not?

Out of experiences like these the realization has grown that the validation of a test is a long *process* rather than a single event. Only through studying the test's correlation with a variety of criteria can we understand just what it is measuring. A series of research studies on the "mechanical aptitude" test, for example, may demonstrate that what it really measures is the ability to carry out finely controlled, skilled movements and that it has nothing to do with the ability to grasp complex relationships of mechanical parts. Thus, it may correlate fairly highly with grades in wood shop, but not with grades in machine shop. It may select competent workers for one factory but not for another.

Therefore, instead of asking the old validity question, "To what extent does this test measure what it purports to measure?" we are now more likely to ask, "*Just what is it that this test does measure?*" Today, we know that we must analyze the content of the test and examine many correlations with different criteria in various groups before we can know the answer. And as we do, our knowledge of what the basic mental *traits* are and how they relate to one another continues to grow and change along with our knowledge of the individual tests themselves. It is not really necessary that a psychologist formulate at the beginning a precise definition of the trait the test will measure. With a general idea about the characteristic and its relationship to either theoretical concepts or practical situations, the psychologist's precision in defining it will increase as the test is tried out in a series of separate research studies.

What are the different types of validity that we must be concerned about in finding out what a test does measure? In the *Standards for Educational and Psychological Tests* (1974), validation procedures are identified as criterion related, construct, and content. Criterion-related validity is empirical in nature and concerned with exploring the relationship between test scores and behavior in specific situations. More simply, performance on a test is empirically checked against some criterion. There are two such types of criterion-related validity—concurrent and predictive. Concurrent validity procedures check the relationship between test scores and current (present) behavior. Thus, concurrent validity is relevant to tests used for diagnosis of existing behavior or current status in the present. Predictive validity procedures look at the relationship between test scores and future behavior. This type of validity is concerned with predicting future outcome. Thus, test scores must be correlated with some future behavior or criterion.

Construct validity is more difficult to define. This type of validity is concerned with the association between test scores and theoretical prediction or some theoretical trait such as intelligence. Construct validity for a test is probably best demonstrated by an accumulation of supportive evidence, from different sources over some period of time, of what the test measures. Evidence showing that a test has some concurrent, predictive, and content validity would be data supporting the notion of construct validity for a test. Construct validity has also been viewed as an accumulation of what is called—by Campbell and Fiske (1959)—convergent and discriminative validity. In other words, in demonstrating construct validity we must show that a test meets theoretical expectations and is associated with variables with which it should be reasonably correlated (convergent validity). At the same time we must show that a test is not related to other variables with which it should not be reasonably correlated. This is referred to as discriminative validity.

Similar to construct validity, content validity is a more subjective type of validity concerned with whether or not a test does cover the material that it purports to cover. The validation procedure involves a systematic examination of the test content to determine if the test represents the behavior base or information area. For example, a test of simple addition would seem to be valid if it was composed of items requiring addition. This type of validity, as you will see, is most important in evaluating achievement tests.

From time to time you will hear about some additional but less meaningful types of validity. These are face validity, internal consistency, and interpretive validity. Face validity is concerned with whether or not the content of a test looks appropriate or good to those people taking or using the test. Not to be confused with content validity, face validity simply pertains to the appropriateness, the relevance, and the attractiveness of the items of the test. Face validity is clearly a favorable characteristic of a test, but it tells us nothing about what a test in fact measures. To look at the internal consistency of a test, we determine if the items of a test discriminate in the same direction as the total score of the test. This procedure involves comparing the performance of the highest scorers on the entire test and the lowest scorers across each of the test items. Items not passed by a reasonable percentage of the high scorers are eliminated. Similar to face validity, internal consistency is a desirable characteristic of a test but in fact does nothing to improve a test's objective validity. Interpretive validity is a subjective yet practical type of validity concerned with the accuracy with which a test is interpreted. In other words, is a test being interpreted accurately and meaningfully to the individuals who have taken it? Unfortunately, little work has been done with the notion of interpretive validity, and in service settings this kind of information is badly needed.

Understanding what is involved in the validation of tests carries three clear implications for test users. One is that if a test is to be employed in making decisions about individuals or groups, all the available evidence should be studied before any attempt is made to interpret the scores. This means that someone in the organization using the test must be capable of making such a study. A "testing program" in schools or in industry can function effectively only when it is run by a thoroughly competent person.

Another implication is that whenever possible, a test to be used for prediction or selection (as of job applicants) should be validated in the specific situation in which it is to be employed. This, of course, requires a special research study on the spot before one begins to use the test routinely to decide which applicants to hire. The relevant validity question to ask when such a study is planned is not "Is the test valid?" but "Will this test add anything to the validity of selection methods now being used?" A college that has been applying definite standards of selection on the basis of high school grades may find that a so-called college aptitude test has nothing to contribute to its program. Another college, with a different program, which draws from a different pool of applicants, may find that the same college aptitude test has considerable validity. Not all situations permit this on-the-spot validation of tests, however. But where it is possible, it is to be highly recommended. For an example of a study of the predictive validity of the Iowa Tests of Educational Development, made especially for high school teachers, see Table 5. It shows, for instance, that tenth graders who score 25 or 26 are likely to succeed in college. Out of every 100 students with scores this high, 91 make at least a 2.0 (C) average, 70 make a 2.5 (C+) average, and 40 make a 3.0 (B) average.

Finally, whether we wish to use tests in practical situations involving individuals or in pure research aimed at increasing our theoretical knowledge of individual differences, we should always remember that our ideas about *what the traits are* as well as what the tests measure must change as new evidence comes in. When research workers fail to get the correlation they expected between "anxiety" and "susceptibility to the stress of failure," they may need to change their views about what is being measured by the anxiety scale they have been using. In addition, they may have to modify their theories about the way personality is affected by the threat of failure. Persons who use special tests a great deal, such as teachers in the public schools, should try to keep abreast of new knowledge about these tests and also about the qualities they measure. Many present-day school teachers, for example, are making decisions about children on the basis of outmoded *concepts* of intelligence. What they need is not just more valid tests but a more penetrating knowledge of what the word intelligence means. We cannot really explore test validity without examining at the same time the validity of our own ideas.

THE MEANING AND TYPES OF RELIABILITY

Validity is the most important consideration in the construction and use of all types of tests. Next in order of importance is *reliability*. In explaining what this is, we can start again with a question: How accurately or how consistently does a test measure whatever it does measure?

When a person takes a test, many things may influence the score, quite apart from the ability or personality trait the test has been designed to measure. When the testee is distracted or re-bellious, he or she may not give as many good answers to questions as when concentrating on the task. This produces a score that is lower than it should be. On the other hand it may happen that the testee encountered the night before, on a television program or in casual conversation, some of the specific questions contained in the test. In this case he or she is likely to obtain a score that is a little higher than customary performance would predict. These are two examples of *chance* influences on test scores. There are innumerable others—emotional reactions to the examiner, temperature and ven-tilation in the examining room, good or bad luck in making guesses about things one really does not know, to mention just a few. They are all essentially unpredictable, and they do not affect all testees in the same way or to the same degree.

What the test maker must discover and communicate to the test users is how inaccurate individual scores are likely to be because of such chance factors. Having this information, those who must inter-pret a score can make the proper allowance for such inaccuracy. Our conclusion about a testee will then follow these lines: Billy is slightly above average in intelligence. There is a 50-50 chance that his IQ lies somewhere between 105 and 115. We will not conclude: Billy has an IQ of 110.

There are a number of ways to analyze the reliability of a test and report the results of the analysis, but most of them have the first step in common: the administration of two versions of the same test to a group of persons whose ages or social characteristics are typical of the people for whom the test is intended. If we want to determine the reliability for 8-year-olds of a particular test of intelligence, we may give a group of 8-year-olds both Form A and Form B simulta-neously. This is called alternate-form reliability. If only one form of a test is available, we can construct separate scoring keys for two halves of the test—usually the odd items on one key, the even items on another—so we obtain for each person two scores rather than one. This is referred to as split-half reliability. If we want to evaluate the

33

Table 5

Some Evidence about the Validity of the Iowa Tests of Educational Development as Measures of Ability to Do College Work

ITED COMPOSITE SCORE (TEST TAKEN IN 10TH GRADE)	CHANCES IN 100 OF EARNING COLLEGE GPA OF			EXPECTED RANGE OF COLLEGE GRADES F D C B A
	2.0	2.5	3.0	
29-30	97	86	62	
27-28	95	80	50	
25-26	91	70	40	
23-24	86	60	29	
21-22	78	49	19	
19-20	60	38	13	
17-18	59	28	8	
15-16	48	19	4	
13-14	38	12	2	
11-12	27	7	1	
9-10	18	4		
7-8	12	2		
5-6	7	1		
3-4	4			
1-2	2			

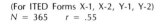

(For ITED Forms X-1, X-2, Y-1, Y-2)
N = 365   r = .55

For students at University of Oregon
and Oregon State College

Most Probable Grade

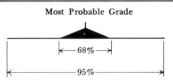

|←—68%—→|

|←——————95%——————→|

of Actual Grades Fall Within These Ranges

From J.S. Carlson and D. W. Fullmer. *College Norms.* Eugene, Ore.: University of Oregon Counseling Center, 1959, p. 11.

reliability of a test of finger dexterity for boys at a vocational school, our procedure will probably be to administer the same test to a group of boys twice, with a short interval between sessions. This procedure, called test-retest reliability, also gives the examiner two scores for each subject. In each example, there is no reason to suppose that all the miscellaneous chance determiners influence both scores the same way. Therefore, we can reason that the more alike the two scores for each person are, the more consistently or reliably, the test is in measuring some nonchance ability or person-ality trait. But the more cases there are in a group of individuals who make very different scores, the more we can suspect that the scores of all testees depend to a large extent on chance factors.

As we saw in Chapter 2, the standard way of stating the degree of resemblance (or difference) between two sets of scores is the correlation coefficient. Because chance influences are always present to some extent, a test maker never finds *perfect* consistency between two sets of scores; that is, the correlation never turns out to be 1.00. But if the test is well constructed and is administered carefully under good conditions, it is not too much to expect that this *re-liability coefficient* should be about .90. For some purposes and in some situations, a test can still be used even though its reliability is considerably lower than this. What is important is that those who make inferences about individuals or groups on the basis of the test *know* how reliable it is so that they can make the necessary allow-ances for inaccuracies.

Unfortunately, describing the reliability of a test by citing the correlation between two versions of it has several disadvantages. The most serious is that a correlation turns out to be higher if there is a great deal of range, or spread, in the scores of the group on which it is based than it does if the members of the group score closer together. Thus, the user, in evaluating the reliability of a test for a certain purpose, should insure that the reliability coefficient is based on a group with about the same amount of diversity as the one being worked with. The Army General Classification Test, for example, is reliable enough to distinguish levels of general mental ability in army recruits, representing as they do an extremely wide variety of natural gifts and educational attainments. But it is not reliable enough to distinguish with any clarity between one college student and another. A psychologist expecting to use this test in a university counseling program would be misled if he or she were to judge its reliability by a coefficient based on data obtained from a group of run-of-the-mill recruits. What is needed is a reliability coefficient based on information pertaining to a group of college students.

Fortunately, there is another way of reporting how accurate or inaccurate scores on a test are: the standard error of measurement (SE_m). We have explained the general meaning of the term standard error in Chapter 2. This particular version of that statistic gives an estimate of the range of variation in a person's score if he or she were to take the same test over and over again an infinite number of times—if, in other words, we could draw many "samples" of the test scores in the testee's whole "population" of scores. This range is a zone of inaccuracy on either side of an obtained score. This range represents limits around the observed score within which we would reasonably expect to find the individual's true score. Stated differently, the standard error of measurement (SE_m) is an estimate of the error made in substituting an observed score for a true score. The SE_m is very useful when interpreting individual scores and may be computed using the following formula:

$$SE_m = SD \sqrt{1 - r}$$

where SD is the standard deviation of the test scores and r the reliability coefficient for the group in which we are interested. For example, if on an intelligence test the standard deviation (SD) is 18 and the reliability (r) of the test is .93, the SE_m of an IQ on this test is:

$$
\begin{aligned}
SE_m &= SD \sqrt{1 - r} \\
&= 18 \sqrt{1 - .93} \\
&= 18 \sqrt{.07} \\
&= 18 \,(.26) \\
SE_m &= 4.6
\end{aligned}
$$

This means that if the SE_m for an intelligence test is 4.6, there is a probability of about two-thirds that an individual's true score is within 4.6 points of the score actually obtained. If Greg gets a score of 154, we can conclude with some assurance that his "true score," free from chance influences, probably lies somewhere between 149.4 and 158.6. This follows from the fact that in any normal distribution, about two-thirds of the cases fall within one standard deviation of the mean. As explained previously, the standard error is a special kind of standard deviation. There is still one chance in three that his "true score" is higher or lower than this, and we can if we wish, using reasoning based on the concept of standard error, say that there is a 5 percent probability that it might even be as low as 145 or as high as 163; this is because, in a normal distribution, about 95 percent of the cases fall within two standard deviations of the mean.

But ordinarily we do not try to make such exact determinations. We use the standard error as a guide to the general amount of inaccuracy we should allow for in interpreting scores and making decisions about individuals. If the intelligence test in the foregoing example is used to select students for an honors program, and the decision has been made that all students who score 155 or higher are eligible, Greg with his score of 154 does not at first glance seem to qualify. But a teacher who takes unreliability into consideration will recognize that Greg may belong in the select group, for the probability is fairly high that his true score is at least 155. In such a case the teacher would look very carefully at various supplementary evidence to find out what kind of student Greg is before deciding whether or not to assign him to the special class. Understanding what reliability means can thus make a real difference in the use of tests in making decisions. (In stressing the fact that tests are not altogether reliable we must always remember that other ways of evaluating people are unreliable too. A test maker tells us how much inaccuracy to allow for. Usually we have no way of knowing how much we should allow for in teachers' judgments, for example.)

For a person who does not understand what test "reliability" means, evaluation of a test may be influenced too strongly by statements about its reliability. For, the word "reliable," as used in our common speech, carries *favorable* connotations—a reliable ("good") man, a reliable ("upstanding") firm, a reliable ("worthwhile") product. Teachers, personnel workers, and clinicians are all too likely to conclude that a reliable test is, *ipso facto*, a *good* test for any purpose they have in mind. Such errors can lead to serious misjudgments of people. Evidence that a test is accurately measuring *something* tells us very little. We need to know much more about the test. Until we know *what* the something it measures is, we are not justified in drawing conclusions about people from the scores they make. As we saw in the previous section, the task of finding out just what a test does measure is long and arduous. "Reliable" does not mean "good" for everything. Validity remains more important than reliability.

NORMS AND DERIVED SCORES

In evaluating tests and interpreting their scores, we must consider, in addition to reliability and validity, the various units in which those scores are expressed. A score that indicates only how many questions a person answered correctly does not tell us very much about the person unless we have some standard of comparison. If

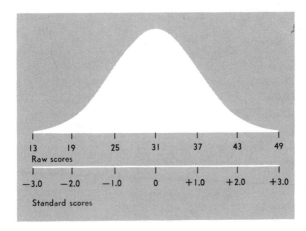

Figure 6. The standard scores corresponding to raw scores at different levels for a distribution in which the mean is 31 and the standard deviation 6.

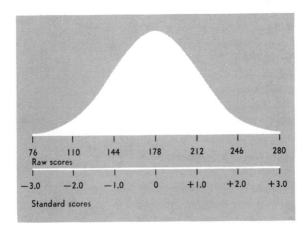

Figure 7. The standard scores corresponding to raw scores at different levels for a distribution in which the mean is 178 and the standard deviation 34.

Leonard brings home a report that his score on a school arithmetic test was 47, the first question his mother is likely to ask is, "What kind of scores did the other children get?" The derived, or transformed, scores used with standardized tests of aptitudes, achievement, and personality are designed to facilitate just such comparison of individual scores with group norms. We can go about the job of deriving, or transforming, scores in several ways.

The simplest way of accomplishing this is to set up *percentile* norms for a group and transform each person's score into an equivalent percentile rank. To construct tables of percentile norms, simply divide by the total number of persons in the group the number of those who rank below each raw score *plus* one-half of those who receive exactly the score in question. If, in the intelligence test example with Greg, 91 out of a class of 100 high school sophomores score below 154, Greg's score of 154 gives him a percentile rank of 91 in this group.

The other common method of translating scores into equivalents that indicate where an individual stands in a group makes use of the mean and standard deviation as a basis for norms. In normal distributions there is a fixed relationship between the distance from the mean and the area under the curve; Figure 6 shows what this relationship is. Regardless of how large or small the standard deviation is in any particular group of scores, it can be used as a meaningful unit of distance along the base line. In a normal distribution, if we measure off one standard-deviation unit from the mean, we find ourselves directly under the point where the curve changes from convex to concave. Three such units measured off from the mean, and we reach a point very near the end of the distribution. Thus, if we wish, we can state in standard-deviation units how far each score is from the mean and indicate in this way where each one fits into the total distribution. Instead of reporting a score as 25 for someone in the group represented in Figure 6, we can report it as -1.0 standard-deviation unit (or -1σ, in the Greek-letter notation often used). As soon as the latter is seen, anyone familiar with the normal distribution curve knows just about how far below average the subject is.

This kind of transformation has enabled psychologists to make comparisons that would not be possible with the raw scores themselves. In another normal distribution of test scores (Figure 7), the mean may be 178 and the standard deviation 34. The numbers along the base line for raw scores are different from those shown in Figure 6, but the standard scores are the same. A score of 144 on this

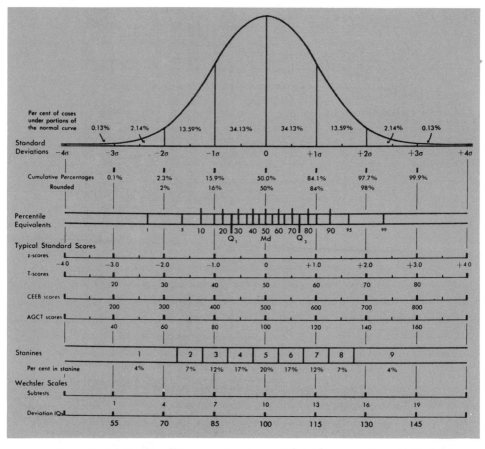

Figure 8. Relationships between various types of derived scores. *(From H. G. Seashore. Methods of Expressing Test Scores. Psychological Corporation Test Service Bulletin, No. 48. New York, 1955.)*

second test (178 minus 34) is just as low as a score of 25 on the first one. Both are reported as −1.0 standard deviation (or −1σ).

For convenience, we often express basic standard scores in many other ways. In order to provide measurements divided into finer units, for instance, we can multiply all numbers by 10 so that they range from −30 to +30 instead of from −3 to +3. Then, in order to eliminate negative scores, we can add 50, so that they range from 20 to 80, with the mean being 50 instead of zero. Neither of these transformations changes in any way the fundamental relationships between scores. In Figure 8 we see how a number of these derived scores as well as the percentile scale are related to the basic normal distribution. Values in vertical alignment on the various horizontal lines beneath the normal curve will be equivalent if the norm groups on which they are based are similar.

In addition to percentile ranks and standard scores, there are various other ways of making scores meaningful. Age and grade norms for school achievement tests require no special explanation. We will consider the IQ in the next chapter.

FAIRNESS

Down through the years, the question of whether mental tests are equally fair to people of different races, nationalities, and social levels has stimulated much discussion and research. In the middle 1960s, when the national spotlight was thrown on the plight of the poor in the United States, this became a major issue. People who use tests as tools of their trade—teachers and school administrators, personnel managers and heads of government agencies—now look for evidence that a test they plan to employ is fair to the people they plan to test, in addition to it being valid, reliable, and suitably normed.

Fairness, like the other concepts explained in this chapter, is a complex matter. Because all human traits are developed through experience, persons whose backgrounds differ widely inevitably react differently to the questions and tasks included in any given test. There is no such thing as a *culture-free* test. What the test constructor or the test user must do, then, is to try the test out on different groups of people who may eventually be asked to take it, and find out not only whether some groups obtain lower average scores than others, but also *how their scores are related to relevant criteria.* If, for example, most members of a minority group tend to score low on an aptitude test designed to predict how successful trainees will be in a particular occupational training program, and the same persons also tend to score low on the criterion measure (so that the correlation between the two sets of scores for this group is .59), the test may be *fair* even though it seems to work against this group. What persons making use of tests for selection purposes must always watch out for, however, are situations in which the *predictive validity* of the test is *not* the same for the minority group as it is for the more typical groups of applicants upon which previous validity studies have been based. If the correlation between test and criterion scores, in the example given above, had turned out to be something like .06 rather than .59, we would have to conclude that the test is not fair to this group of applicants, regardless of how valid it has proved to be for other groups. The only way of making sure that a test one proposes to use to assess the ability of a new kind of applicant is fair to people in this group is to run some extra studies relating test scores to performance.

When test validities do turn out to be reasonably high for a "disadvantaged" group, the test can be a useful tool to help *counteract* discrimination and open up opportunities for individuals. Tests can often serve as a means of *discovering* talent in cases where without tests it might have been overlooked because of conscious or unconscious prejudice in the minds of interviewers against applicants who are black or brown, poor or shabbily dressed. In considering test fairness we should keep in mind the fact that other methods of judging people's capabilities are just as likely to be unfair as tests are—perhaps even a little more likely.

Sometimes it is also important to know how a new test is related to other tests for a different population of testees, so that through procedures like factor analysis, the nature of the ability structure in this group can be clarified. In short, separate judgments of the fairness of a given test must be made for various groups and various testing purposes. We shall return to this concept in later chapters where we are concerned with particular varieties of tests.

CLASSIFICATION OF TESTS

In order to consider the principles and techniques of psychological testing in more detail, it is necessary to classify tests under a few major headings. There is no altogether satisfactory way of doing this, but the most generally acceptable categorization is based on what the tests are designed to measure. The most fundamental distinction separates *ability* tests, by means of which one determines what a person can do, from *personality* tests, by means of which one determines what a person feels, wants, or worries about. Under the first of these headings, it is convenient to distinguish between intelligence tests and tests of more limited varieties of ability.

In this chapter we have considered certain concepts and procedures applicable to all kinds of tests. There are other concepts and procedures that apply to one of the three areas—intelligence, special abilities, or personality—more than to the others. We shall take these up in the chapters that follow.

Intelligence
Tests

4

The attempt to measure human intelligence has entailed more continuous, long-term, intensive effort than any other project in psychological measurement. In the study of intelligence, philosophical curiosity interacts with practical demands. For centuries thinkers have puzzled over the enormous differences in sheer intellectual capacity that separate a Socrates from an ordinary citizen, an idiot from a normal child. They have asked whether such differences are innate or acquired—whether biological or educational factors are more influential in producing them. Eventually, because of the practical needs of civilized societies, it became more and more urgent to find some way to evaluate the intelligence of individuals as accurately as possible. The advent of universal education brought all sorts of children, talented and untalented, into the schools. Some appeared to be incapable of mastering the curriculum educators had planned for them. Others raced through it and busied themselves with scientific experiments and philosophical speculations long before they reached physical maturity. Clearly, teachers needed to be able to distinguish between different mental capacities in order to educate children suitably. Similar problems arose in military organizations and in industries in connection with attempts to fit individuals into appropriate positions.

When psychologists began their effort to measure intelligence, just before the beginning of the twentieth century, they lacked a precise idea of the nature of this quality. As we saw in the discussion of validity in the previous chapter, this situation is not unusual, nor is it necessarily detrimental. Even a vague idea about a human trait can serve to guide a test maker in selecting test items and planning validity studies. Then as evidence accumulates about what the test scores *are related to*, the test maker is able to formulate increasingly clearer definitions of what the test measures and to modify and improve the test.

The first intelligence test for children, the Binet-Simon scale, was preceded by a long period during which Binet had carefully observed differences in the thinking processes of children. He studied his own little daughters, talked to teachers about how they judged mental capacity, and carried out various experiments before he was ready to present an intelligence test to the public. This work gave Binet certain clues about what an intelligence test should be. First of all, he decided, it should reflect the rapid growth in mental capacity that occurs during childhood. Second, for practical reasons if for no other, it should tap the characteristics by which teachers differentiate between "bright" and "dull" children in their schoolrooms. His tentative definition of intelligence as measured by this first scale was "the tendency to take and maintain a definite direction; the capacity to make adaptations for the purpose of attaining a desired end; and the power of auto-criticism." As mentioned earlier, the publication of an intelligence test at this particular time was stimulated by a request from the Paris school authorities for a method that would help differentiate between really dull children and others who were just lazy.

The idea caught on immediately. The Binet-Simon Scale itself went through two revisions, in 1908 and in 1911, and it was translated and adapted in many countries. In the United States, Lewis M. Terman of Stanford University took up the idea and started working on an American revision. The result was the Stanford-Binet test, first published in 1916, revised in 1937, brought up to date in 1960, and in 1972 the norms were updated and improved with a more representative sample, but the test content was not changed. For half a century the Stanford-Binet test constituted a virtually official standard for intelligence measurement, like the bars and weights in Washington that officially define for us our foot and pound. At present, however, more alternative tests are available than in previous years, and the tendency to refer all of intelligence measurement to the Stanford-Binet has diminished. But the part this test played in the development of theoretical concepts and practical applications of mental testing can hardly be overemphasized.

DISTINGUISHING FEATURES OF BINET TESTS

Although the successive revisions differed from one another and from the original Binet-Simon test, there is a body of features that characterize all versions. First, they are *scales*. This means that the constituent questions and tasks are grouped on the basis of their difficulty. Beginning with easy questions, the examiner asks harder and harder ones as the test proceeds. A score chiefly depends on how far up this ladder the child can go, rather than on how fast or how fluent he or she is (though both speed and fluency are required in some of the individual tests). From Binet's 1908 revision on, the tests have been grouped by *age levels*. A great deal of effort has been expended on the task of finding out just what the age norms are. In order to assign a test to a particular age level, it is necessary to investigate how children of various ages handle it. The tests pegged at year 10, for example, must contain tasks that are in the scope of only a minority of 9-year-olds, a majority of 10-year-olds, and a much larger number of 11-year-olds. Thus, an intelligence scale of the Binet type is built to measure *mental growth*.

The second shared feature of the Binet tests is that they yield a general *global* measure of intelligence rather than an analysis of separate special abilities. It is clear from Binet's definition that he thought of intelligence as a complex capacity for handling a great array of tasks rather than a sum of distinct abilities to do particular things. In keeping with this view, the tests for a single age level may require knowledge of words, perception of details in pictures, reasoning, and immediate memory. No attempt is made to segregate types of ability. (Figure 9, p. 47 which shows the variety of materials used in administering the 1960 Stanford-Binet test, gives some idea of this diversity.)

The third characteristic that distinguishes Binet-type tests from many others is that they are designed to be given *individually* by a skilled examiner (see Figure 10, p. 49). It requires more skill than one might suppose to maintain a friendly, encouraging attitude toward the testee, while simultaneously carrying out instructions to the letter. And these instructions are rigid. For example, the examiner must never change the wording of a question in any way—what might seem to be a minor modification may have the effect of making an item harder or easier than it was for the subjects on whom the age norms rest. The examiner may praise the testee in order to stimulate best efforts, but not too often or at the wrong times. Some questions may be repeated, but not others. If it is not clear whether an answer meets the specifications for a given age

Figure 9. Materials used in testing intelligence with the Stanford-Binet. *(By permission, Houghton Mifflin Company.)*

level, the examiner may ask a question, but must be sure not to give the testee a clue to the right answer. To act natural, friendly, and relaxed while using procedures and words that are so rigidly specified requires a great deal of practice. Obviously, a Binet test cannot be given by just anyone who comes into possession of the materials.

Finally, the system of scoring in all Binet tests is tied to the *age norms*. Mental age, usually abbreviated MA, indicates the age group for which the child's performance would be typical. For example, an MA of 9-6 means that a child is as far along in general mental development as the average 9½-year old.

THE MEANING OF THE IQ

The Stanford-Binet and other Binet-type tests also provide for the computation of an *intelligence quotient* (IQ). Until the 1960 revision, when statistical refinements were introduced, the IQ was figured simply by dividing the child's mental age by chronological age, then multiplying the quotient by 100 to eliminate the decimal point. For example, a child whose MA is 10, but whose actual chronological age (CA) is 9 would have an IQ of 111 (10/9 × 100). The IQ tells us something about the child's *rate* of mental growth up to the time of the test.

Unfortunately, the term IQ became overly popular and was used in numerous unwarranted ways. Misconceptions about its meaning are still common. It is *not* the all-important index of intellectual capacity it is often assumed to be. And it is *not* a measure of an *amount* of anything, but simply a way of indicating what a child's average growth rate has been. At one stage in the research on intelligence it was thought that growth rates would be stable enough throughout childhood to serve as a basis for accurate predictions of adult intelligence. But as more knowledge accumulated, it became apparent that the "constancy of the IQ" is far from absolute.

For one thing, even in tests that are standardized and allocated to age levels as carefully as they were in the 1937 revision of the Stanford-Binet scale, IQ's at different age levels are not entirely comparable statistically. A very bright child could obtain a higher IQ at 12 than at 6, even if the child's growth rate had not changed at all, simply because the variability of the IQ distribution was greater for 12-year-olds than for 6-year-olds. In other, less carefully standardized tests, this variation in the meaning of high and low IQ's from age to age is even more troublesome.

Another inadequacy is that the IQ is not an appropriate way to describe *adult* intelligence. Like physical growth, mental growth in adults lacks the predictable regularity it shows in children. From the mid-teens on, *age* standards are relatively meaningless. It makes no sense to say that 20-year-old Jim's mental age is 25, because 25-year-olds and 20-year-olds do not differ in their response to the material in intelligence tests. What looks like an IQ for an adult is really a standard score. It signifies that the person occupies the same position in the adult distribution as a child with that IQ would occupy in a similar distribution of children. As psychologists studied the complexities of IQ scores, they came to realize that *all* IQ's, for children as well as for adults, could be interpreted as standard scores. What an individual IQ really tells us is how many standard deviations above or below average a person is.

One of the most useful things a student can learn is not to pay too much attention to a numerical IQ. Many first-rate standardized tests now provide norm tables from which other derived scores may be obtained—scores that show directly where a person stands in a group with which he or she wishes to be compared; for example, 7-year-olds, high school graduates, or army recruits. The 1960 revision

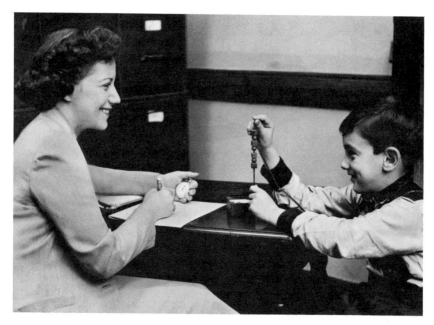

Figure 10. The administration of the Stanford-Binet test. *(From the City College of New York Educational Clinic.)*

of the Stanford-Binet test, while it continues to employ IQ terminology, no longer provides for the computation of this score in the old way—that is, by dividing MA by CA. Instead, the examiner uses tables that show directly how different a child's score is from the mean, or average, of a representative group of children the same age. This derived scores is *called* an IQ but is really a standard score. The IQ concept served us well in the early days of intelligence testing, but it is now being retired from active service.

THE WECHSLER TESTS

Besides Lewis M. Terman, who devised the original Stanford-Binet test, and Maud Merrill, who worked with him on the 1937 revision and prepared the 1960 revision, another American has been particularly important in intelligence measurement—David Wechsler. In 1939, Wechsler published a standardized set of individual intelligence tests designed especially for adults. It was called the Wechsler-Bellevue Scale (the second part of the name honored New York's Bellevue Hospital where Wechsler worked). This test imme-

diately came into wide use because of the demand, with the un-
precedented growth of clinical psychology during and after World
War II, for the evaluation of intellectual ability in millions of adults.
The Binet scale in its various revisions had met the needs of institutions serving children, but had never been entirely satisfactory with
adults.

Since World War II, Wechsler has developed a scale for children built on the same plan as the original Wechsler—Bellevue
Scale. In 1955 the adult scale was revised and in 1974 the scale for
children received a much needed revision. A third addition to the
family occurred in 1967 when Wechsler developed a children's preschool scale designed for ages 4 to 6½ years. A number of subtests
on this scale are downward extensions and adaptations of the subtests on the children's scale. The three current versions of Wechsler's
tests, then, are the WAIS (Wechsler Adult Intelligent Scale), published in 1955, the WISC-R (Wechsler Intelligence Scale for Children,
Revised), published in 1974, and the WPPSI (Wechsler Preschool and
Primary Scale of Intelligence) published in 1967. Although the WAIS
and the WISC-R overlap to some degree, the WAIS is principally
designed for ages 16 and above, the WISC-R for ages 15 and below.
The infant in the family (WPPSI) is designed for ages 4 to 6½.

Wechsler includes many of the same kinds of questions and
tasks that Binet, Terman, and others had used, but he combines them
differently. Instead of grouping them by age levels, he assembles
them by type of question or task, arranging the specific items within
each set according to difficulty. For example, all the arithmetic
questions are in one subtest, all the block-design tasks in another.
The subtests in turn are grouped into two main classes labeled
Verbal and *Performance*. The verbal tests included in the WAIS are
headed Information, Comprehension, Digit Span, Similarities, Arithmetic, and Vocabulary. The performance tests are titled Picture Ar-
rangement, Picture Completion, Block Design, Object Assembly, and
Digit Symbol. (The subtests in the WISC-R are similar, with a few
minor changes). The *Verbal* tests require the testee to explain what
words mean, give correct answers to informational questions like
"What is the capital of Norway?," and work simple arithmetical
problems in his head. Figure 11 p. 51 shows a person working on the
Block Design test from the *Performance* scale.

When the WISC was revised in 1974, adult-oriented items were
replaced with items more consistent with childhood experiences.
Other changes included the elimination of items that may tend to be
more familiar to certain groups of children and the addition of
females and blacks in the pictorial items of subtests. The administration and scoring procedures were improved and some subtests were

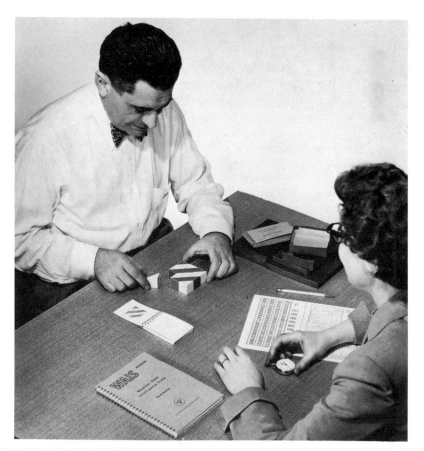

Figure 11. Samples of material used in testing intelligence with the WAIS. *(From the Psychological Corporation.)*

lengthened in order to improve reliability. In sum, the WISC-R, revised after 25 years, appears to be a meaningful, useful, and worthy successor to the WISC.

Wechsler has set up separate norms for each subtest. It is thus possible to see how an adult or child compares in each category with a group that is representative of the whole population. Further, we can add up the standard scores on the separate subtests to produce on overall verbal score, an overall performance score, and a total score. Finally, by comparing these three inclusive scores against norm tables for the subject's age we can read off the verbal perform-ance, and total "IQ's." Such an IQ, however, like that obtained from the 1960 Terman-Merrill revision, is not an actual *quotient* of MA and CA. It is, instead, an indication in standard-deviation units of how the person relates to the average of his or her age distribution.

(See Figure 8 for the relationship between Wechsler IQ's and the basic standard-deviation units in many other systems of derived scores.)

When these scales first became available it was hoped that differences among scores on the separate subtests would facilitate diagnostic evaluations of mental functioning that would be helpful to clinicians and teachers interested in knowing more about an individual than an overall score revealed. It seemed possible that an analysis of strengths and weaknesses shown on the various tests could help to answer such specific questions as: In which psychiatric classification does Mr. King belong? Has Mrs. Logan incurred some kind of brain damage? What particular educational deficiencies are handicapping Susan? As time has passed, however, statements about the diagnostic significance of score patterns, or profiles, have become more and more guarded. We know now that there are many possible reasons why Mr. Henderson may, for instance, score lower on *Arithmetic* than on the other tests. Such a discrepancy may indicate anxiety, but it may simply mean that the subject never really learned elementary arithmetic in the first place. Clinicians still study a testee's score profile and answers to specific questions, seeking clues to help understand the individual; but they have learned to regard the ideas generated in this way as mere *hypotheses* to be checked against other information about the person.

Differences between verbal and performance scores are more meaningful than discrepancies between the scores on particular subtests. True, we must be cautious in interpreting these differences as well. Neither scale is so reliable or accurate that *small* disparities should be taken seriously. But if a person turns out to be 15 points or more higher on one scale than on the other (15 points is the standard deviation of the IQ distribution for the Wechsler tests), it may be useful to try to account for this discrepancy and to consider what it may mean in planning the person's future—whether this planning has to do with clinical treatment, educational undertakings, or occupational placement. It is clear, in the first place, that the verbal scale is more closely related to schooling than the performance scale is. A combination of low verbal score and much higher performance score often reflects some educational deficiency. The verbal score also *predicts* far more accurately than the performance score how successful a person is likely to be in future school situations. Besides this difference in the influence of formal schooling, many other factors may be responsible for inequalities between the two halves of the test. When examiners encounter such discrepancies they look for evidence—in the examinees' records, in what they say about themselves, or in what others say about them—that will perhaps account for the discrepancies and will help those who must deal with these individuals to understand them better. In the report on a person's test results, the examiner regularly includes not just the scores but some qualitative analysis of what the scores may mean.

In general, however, the most valuable information obtained from either the Stanford-Binet or the Wechsler test is an evaluation of overall intellectual level. Analyses of the correlations between different subtests have shown that a large general factor runs through them all. Binet's belief that intelligence is not the sum of many simpler abilities, but rather an overall quality that inheres in various kinds of complex thinking is supported by much research evidence. It is still reasonable to assume that there is such a thing as *general* mental ability, and that we can evaluate it by trying a person out on a variety of questions and tasks. And it is not incompatible with this view to assume that there are also such things as special abilities and talents, but that probably neither the Binet nor the Wechsler test is designed to measure them very efficiently.

GROUP TESTS OF INTELLIGENCE

We have gone into some detail about the two leading *individual* tests of intelligence because the basic concepts and issues are more clearly defined for them than they are for group tests. But as for frequency of use, group tests rank far ahead of individual tests, millions of them being given each year in schools, industries, and military organizations. Thus it is essential that the educated citizen know enough about them to interpret their results intelligently.

Although group intelligence tests are similar in many ways to individual tests, there are some critical differences. Each particular group test is more *limited* in purpose than is an individual test like the Binet or Wechsler. It may be intended for a single age or grade group, for instance, and be inappropriate for much younger or older children. Often, related tests for successive age levels are published as a series. There are four Henmon-Nelson Tests, for example, one for Grades 3–6, one for Grades 6–9, one for Grades 9–12, and one for Grades 13–17. Group tests differ in types of questions, too. One designed especially for selecting promising college students, such as the Scholastic Aptitude Test of the College Entrance Examination Board, is vastly different in content from a group test designed for sorting army recruits into various training programs, such as the Army General Classification Test.

Such specificity is an advantage in particular situations. As a rule, an appropriate group test predicts specific criterion scores more successfully than individual tests do. If we wish to know ahead of time the likely first-year grade averages of applicants to a certain college, it would be of no advantage to give each person an individual WAIS test. Scores on the verbal half of this test do predict college grades fairly well, but scores on any one of the special college aptitude tests predict them even better—and the latter can be administered with a fraction of the time and expense involved in individual testing.

What advantages, then, do individual tests have over group tests? First of all, they allow the examiner to get a better idea of how highly motivated the testee is, and to encourage the individual to put out a greater effort. There is always the possibility that a score on a group test constitutes an extreme underestimate of individual ability, if for some reason the testee was not trying to answer the questions correctly. Secondly, an individual test gives a sounder indication of the mental capacities of persons whose reading skills are not as well developed as their ability to think and reason. Although there are some nonverbal group tests, those most commonly used do penalize nonreaders. Thirdly, individual tests afford an opportunity for qualitative study and observation. An examiner is more likely to be able to describe the way a child thinks and suggest some possible reasons for the child's deficiencies after a Wechsler or Stanford-Binet test than after a group test.

A person who knows group tests well has a great variety to choose from. There are extremely difficult tests that challenge the thinking of advanced graduate students and very easy ones suitable for the mentally retarded. There are tests based almost entirely on language and others in which no language of any sort is used either in the items themselves or in the directions. There are tests which yield only a single total score and tests designed to give a differentiated profile of scores. To consider all these types separately would be beyond our concerns here. All we need to note now is that in one way or another they all enable us to compare the general mental ability of an individual with the average of some group to which the person belongs or with which the person must compete.

INFANT TESTS

One field of research within the general area of intelligence testing deserves special attention because the results obtained are quite untypical. This anomaly is the testing of infants and very young children. All the tests we have been talking about are designed primarily for children of school age and for adults. The Stanford-Binet, which reaches down to a lower age level than the others, does include a group of questions for 2-year-olds and has been widely used in preschool testing, but it is not suitable for children younger than 2, or even for *dull* 2-year-olds. The question inevitably arises: Is it possible to find out how bright a child is before he or she reaches this age? It would be very helpful for some practical purposes, such as placing children in foster homes, as well as for many research purposes, if such measurements could be made.

There have, in fact, been several well-planned studies of what babies of different ages typically can do. Several infant scales have been developed that enable us to determine how advanced in development any particular child is. In administering such a test, an examiner may, for example, present a ring to a 3-month old baby and observe whether or not the infant reaches for it. The examiner may listen to the babbling of a 9-month-old to find out whether the baby can say "da-da" or something equally complex. While the second example would seem to evaluate a rudimentary sort of language development, the largest proportion of the items on infant scales reflect sensory-motor skills.

Such standardized tests of infant development have turned out to be helpful in measuring a child's status *at the time of the test.* They are useful to pediatricians and others who deal with very young children and who need to be able to base their treatments and recommendations on an infant's developmental rather than chronological age. At any age level some children are more advanced than others.

Evidence has piled up, however, that such infant tests do *not* predict how rapid a child's *later* intellectual development will be. The child who is slow about sitting up alone and reaching for objects on the table may be the first student in class to learn to read or to master the intricacies of long division. Except for cases of extreme mental retardation, it is not possible to estimate what a child's later IQ is going to be from any sort of test given during the child's first year.

DIRECTIONS OF PROGRESS
IN INTELLIGENCE TESTING

One way of describing what intelligence tests measure is the ability to deal with *symbols.* Thinking, in which symbols rather than objects themselves are manipulated, is an essential component of civilized life. The more intelligent a person is, the more complex and abstract these symbols can be. As they grow to maturity, children increase their capacity for symbolic thinking and also tend to become *specialized* in the kind of symbols they can deal with most adequately. The ability to measure this capacity has therefore been of great value.

Useful as intelligence tests have been, however, they are not an unmixed blessing. For one thing, erroneous and outmoded ideas about what they measure tend to persist and give rise to unjustified conclusions about individuals. Tested intelligence is a more *limited* trait than people often interpret it to be. The IQ is not an index of general human *quality*. It does not tell how "gifted" a person is in art, music, mechanics, or human understanding. It does not show how well the person will adapt to new situations. It does not indicate how rapidly or easily the person will learn new things in the many kinds of nonschool situations. Most important of all, it is not a pure measure of *innate* capacity, but reflects experience as well as potential, education as well as aptitude.

Continuing efforts to improve the practice of intelligence testing have proceeded in several directions. Some psychologists have been most interested in breaking down the global concept of general intelligence into narrower concepts of special kinds of intellectual ability. As they proceeded with their study of primary mental abilities they discovered that a much larger number of these could be differentiated than they had expected. Louis L. Thurstone's work in the 1930s led to usable tests of verbal ability, spatial ability, perceptual speed, memory, reasoning, and several other varieties of intelligence. J. P. Guilford's continuation of this line of research in the years since then indicates that there are 120 or more distinguishable varieties of mental ability. Separate tests of many of these have been made available, at least for research purposes.

One line of research upon which special interest has been focused is the measurement of *creativity*. This calls for tests in which the questions do not have specified "right answers," but rather invite subjects to think of *many* alternative answers or produce *new* and original responses. For example, one test asks the person to write unusual uses of some common object, such as a tin can or a newspaper. Another requires the person to think of clever titles for pictures. It is not altogether clear that children who do well on such tasks are those who will later become creative thinkers and artists, but there is considerable evidence that such children are different kinds of people from those who typically get the best scores on ordinary intelligence tests. Thus it seems very much worth while to identify them and find out more about their development.

Still another new direction in intelligence testing is the construction of tests that teachers can use to *stimulate* intellectual development in young children. One especially influential set of research-based ideas about the stages through which children pass and the kinds of experience that enable them to move from one stage to the next is contained in the many books published by the Swiss psychologist Jean Piaget. There have been several attempts to develop an intelligence scale based on Piaget's concepts. *Let's Look at First Graders, Written Exercises for First Graders, and Instructional and Assessment Materials for First Graders*, prepared by Educational Testing Service for the New York City schools, are materials of this sort. The first of these publications is a guide for teachers, telling them what kinds of things to look for in children as evidence of the sorts of development they should be trying to facilitate. Figure 12 shows what these are. The other two publications, along with accompanying materials, provide both practice exercises and assessment techniques. There are no norms, scores, or IQ's, although many of the exercises resemble those used in ordinary intelligence tests. An example is shown in Figure 13 p. 58. The plan is to stimulate each child to move as rapidly as possible up an individual developmental ladder rather than to compare one child's attainments with those of other children.

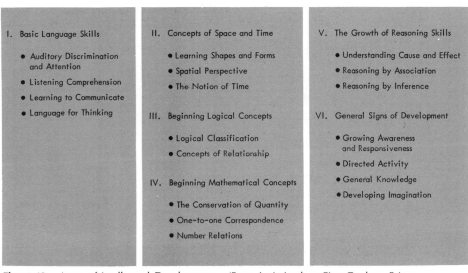

I. Basic Language Skills

    • Auditory Discrimination and Attention

    • Listening Comprehension

    • Learning to Communicate

    • Language for Thinking

II. Concepts of Space and Time

    • Learning Shapes and Forms

    • Spatial Perspective

    • The Notion of Time

III. Beginning Logical Concepts

    • Logical Classification

    • Concepts of Relationship

IV. Beginning Mathematical Concepts

    • The Conservation of Quantity

    • One-to-one Correspondence

    • Number Relations

V. The Growth of Reasoning Skills

    • Understanding Cause and Effect

    • Reasoning by Association

    • Reasoning by Inference

VI. General Signs of Development

    • Growing Awareness and Responsiveness

    • Directed Activity

    • General Knowledge

    • Developing Imagination

Figure 12. Areas of Intellectual Development. *(From* Let's Look at First Graders. *Princeton, N.J.: Educational Testing Service, 1965.)*

Figure 13. Items from *Written Exercises for First Graders* *(Princeton, N.J.: Educational Testing Service, 1965).* The child's task is to select the picture that does not fit in with the others, thus indicating that the concept involved is understood.

With all their faults, intelligence tests are indispensable tools in modern society. We use them to help us make decisions about the placement of individuals for school and work, and to help us formulate educational and social policies. As research on intelligence tests has continued, they have become sharper and more adaptable. But like all tools they require skillful handling and thorough knowledge of what they will and will not do.

Tests of
Special Ability

5

APTITUDE AND ACHIEVEMENT

Even the most casual observation of people is enough to show us that intelligence is not all that counts toward success. Bill Jenkins does extremely well in college science courses even though he had only an average rating on the intelligence test he took as an entering freshman. But he has studied science and mathematics diligently since he was 12, thereby accumulating a vast amount of specific knowledge and mastering the essential problem-solving skills. Henry Harlow becomes an outstanding machinist because he possesses to an unusual degree the ability to see how parts fit together. Joe McGee shows an amazing sensitivity to fine differences in pitch and rhythm and makes use of this talent in learning to play the violin. Lucille Rosen knows far more about contemporary affairs and international relations than anyone else in her high school class and thus becomes the natural candidate to represent her school at an international conference. We could multiply examples of special fitness endlessly.

Psychologists have proceeded along two different lines in developing tests to identify such special talents. These two undertakings, achievement testing and aptitude testing, at first followed somewhat different courses, but eventually the traffic on the two highways merged. It is still customary for writers on mental testing to distinguish between aptitude and achievement tests, but the distinction has become more a matter of convenience than of basic concepts.

59

The terms *aptitude* and *achievement* still carry erroneous connotations arising from historical sources. In earlier periods *aptitude* usually meant special talents presumably based on innate, or hereditary, differences among persons rather than on differences due to experience and learning. To say a child had a high degree of musical aptitude meant that the child possessed the kind of ear and brain that would facilitate learning of complex musical skills, not that he or she possessed some of these skills already. Intelligence, as measured by the tests considered in the previous chapter, was considered to be a special kind of "innate" aptitude for school work. An early book on aptitude testing by Johnson O'Connor was actually entitled *Born That Way.*

Achievement tests, on the other hand, were thought to measure what individuals had *learned.* The search for more reliable and valid achievement tests was stimulated by the demand for better and more convenient school examinations—in many school situations it is important to obtain an accurate estimate of how much a given student really knows about algebra, English literature, or chemistry. Various special achievement tests were also constructed for nonschool situations, such as trade tests to enable an employment interviewer to find out whether a person claiming to be a skilled worker really belongs in the "skilled" category.

As has already been pointed out, psychologists no longer think intelligence tests measure pure "innate" ability; rather, they measure an unanalyzable mixture of inborn potential and educational experience. This conclusion holds for other varieties of aptitude test. The ability measured by mechanical-aptitude tests, for example, is partly an outgrowth of mechanical experience. The ability measured by clerical-aptitude is partly an outgrowth of whatever experiences have sharpened a person's perception of fine details, and that measured by musical-aptitude tests is partly a reflection of musical training. In practice we cannot disentangle the "natural" from the "acquired" components of aptitude, although we can think about them separately if we like.

Furthermore, in practical studies designed to produce tests of aptitude for particular kinds of work or training, an achievement test often turns out to be the best predictor of future success in the field in question. Thus, tests measuring what a student knows about subjects taught in high school—English, mathematics, science, history, and so on—are used successfully to assess aptitude for college work. A measure of flying information was a valuable part of the test battery used to select Air Force pilots. Spelling tests have been useful in selecting clerical workers.

What then is the distinction between aptitude and achievement tests? Besides the fact that the two varieties of tests have different *histories*, the main distinction is a matter of *purpose*. Tests developed and used primarily to select workers or trainees are labeled aptitude tests; those used primarily to find out how much students have learned are called achievement tests. The more general term "ability" covers both.

Among the tests we ordinarily classify as aptitude measures are those that resulted from well-known major research programs. A large-scale investigation of mechanical aptitude at the University of Minnesota, completed in 1930 by Donald G. Paterson and his coworkers, produced three tests that have been in constant use since that time: the Minnesota Spatial Relations Test, the Minnesota Mechanical Assembly Test, and the Minnesota Paper Form Board. At about the same time, another extensive research undertaking at the University of Iowa produced the Seashore Measures of Musical Talents. Other examples could be given, but these two are sufficient to illustrate the historical reasons why certain tests are usually put in the aptitude category today. Other research studies contributed clerical-aptitude tests, methods for identifying artistic talent, and measures of dexterity and motor coordination. For the most part, such tests have been classed as aptitude rather than achievement measures.

More useful at present, however, than this distinction based on research history is the distinction based on purpose. If we plan to use a test chiefly as a *predictor* of how well individuals will perform in some area, we can consider it an aptitude test, regardless of how its author classifed it. If we plan to use it mainly to *evaluate* an individual's accomplishments or adequacy of education and experience, it is for our purposes an achievement test, even if its author did not think of it in this way. The two purposes are not exclusive of one another, of course. We may wish to evaluate and to predict for the same person, and the same test may well be useful for both purposes.

VALIDITY FOR DIFFERENT PURPOSES

The advantage of this approach to special abilities lies in its clarifying our thinking about the evidence we must have to prove that a test is really valid. What we are interested in is validity *for specific purposes.* We must make sure that the evidence the author presents for the validity of the test is really relevant to these ends; just any kind of validity coefficient is not enough. For example, if the author of a test of mechanical comprehension reports that the scores of a group of ninth-grade boys in January correlate to the extent of .65 with independent ratings of these same boys made by their instructor during the same January, we still know nothing about the test's *predictive* validity. If our purpose is to select promising students for a technical high school, we need to find some evidence that the test has actually been given to a similar group of boys *before* they entered high school, and that these early scores showed reasonably high correlations with *later* evaluations.

In Figure 14 we see the outcome of a special predictive study of a battery of tests used to select Air Force trainees during World War

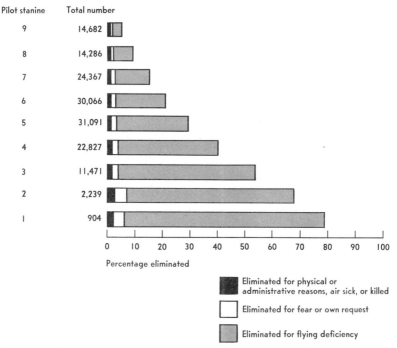

Figure 14. Percentage of candidates eliminated from primary pilot training as related to stanine scores on the selection battery. *(From "Psychological Activities in the Training Command, Army Air Forces," by the Staff, Psychological Section, Fort Worth, Texas, in* Psychological Bulletin. *Washington, D.C.: American Psychological Association, Inc., 1945.)*

II. (The *stanine* is a standard score—"standard nine"—in which 5 is average, 1 is low, and 9 is high. It is shown along with other derived scores in Figure 8.) The results turned out to be clear and unambiguous, so that the subsequent use of this set of tests to select pilots was plainly justified. The figures showed that admitting only candidates with high stanines would reduce to a minimum the proportion of men who washed out during primary training.

If we intend to use a test to measure achievement rather than aptitude, a different kind of validity evidence becomes relevant. The main question is whether the *content* of the test really samples the subject matter in question. We can tell something about this by examining the questions. But we also need information about *how* the items included in the test were selected and *who* did the selecting. For example, a high school teacher decides to use a standardized achievement test at the end of a course in American history. The teacher obtains a sample of a test that appears suitable, along with a manual of information about it. If the teacher knows the authors of this test, at least by reputation, and respects their judgment about the objectives of an American history course, he or she starts out with a favorable attitude. If the manual reports that a committee of experts drew up the preliminary outline and served as consultants in cases of doubtful items, the teacher is further impressed. If the authors tried out the first set of items on a representative group of students to make sure that the meanings of the questions were clear and that they were neither too hard nor too easy, another point is chalked up in favor of the test.

To summarize, then, an ability test can be considered either an aptitude or an achievement test, depending on the purpose for which we desire to use it. If it is to be used as an aptitude test, *predictive* validity must be demonstrated. If it is to be used as an achievement test, *content* validity is important.

RESEARCH ON SPECIAL ABILITIES

Occupational Studies

One of the major goals of the early aptitude testers was to produce the tools that would make possible scientific vocational guidance. This hope has been dimmed somewhat as time has passed. Aptitudes, it seems, are more complex, more dependent on special kinds of previous experience, than we first thought they were. Many special talents have turned out not to be measurable at all, at least by present procedures. Then, too, interests and abilities often differ widely, so that individuals have no wish to enter occupations in line with their measured aptitudes. Finally, technological change has become so rapid that we have no assurance that a test showing high predictive validity for a particular occupation in 1970 will be related to anything people are doing in 1980. There is, however, some sound evidence that people in different occupations do differ from one another in their special abilities. The average scores for garage mechanics and clerical workers on several tests are shown in Figure 15. Clerical workers, it seems, are well above garage mechanics in educational ability (what is usually called general intelligence), clerical ability as measured by a number-checking test, and three kinds of dexterity. Garage mechanics, however, are higher in both tests of mechanical ability. On the basis of evidence like this it is often possible for a vocational counselor to tell clients whether they have the same pattern of abilities as other people in an occupation being considered, even though the counselor is not able to predict just how successful a client would be on the job.

A large-scale study by Robert L. Thorndike and Elizabeth P. Hagen, reported in the book *10,000 Careers*, gives us some additional confirmation that occupational groups do indeed differ in patterns of abilities. It also indicates, however, that the degree of success a person will attain within an occupation cannot be predicted from test scores. What Thorndike and Hagen did was first, to locate in 1955 as many as possible of the men who had taken the Air Force battery of tests during a certain period in 1943 (more than 10,000 in all), and next to find out what occupation each man had gone into. They then assessed by a variety of methods—such as salary, advancement, professional qualifications—how successful each had been in his work. The profiles of average scores for different occupational groups varied widely, as Figure 16 demonstrates. But the correlations between success ratings in the various occupations and scores on the tests were almost all in the near-zero range.

In applying such findings to individual cases, we must remember that the scores plotted in Figures 15 and 16 are *averages*. Within each occupation, individuals vary greatly. Some manage to meet the demands of a job with far less of a given ability than the average worker possesses, others have much more. Since most work can be done in a variety of ways, individuals perhaps use different aptitudes in accomplishing their tasks. This is particularly true of more demanding occupations. However, there are probably limits to this interchangeability, and a worker *too* low on some essential aptitude

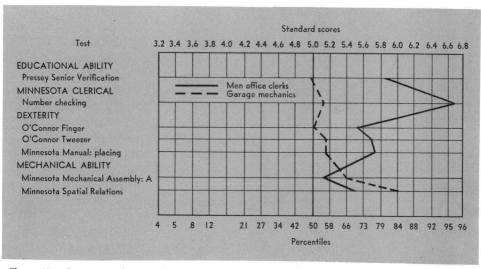

Figure 15. Occupational test profiles for clerical workers and garage mechanics. *(From B. J. Dvorak. Differential Occupational Ability Patterns. Employment Stabilization Research Institute, Vol. 3, No. 8. Minneapolis: University of Minnesota Press. Copyright 1935 by the University of Minnesota.)*

may not be able to handle a job even if he has many other vocational assets. Thus, a rough sorting process seems to go on constantly in the world of work, one that could produce the patterning we see in Figures 15 and 16.

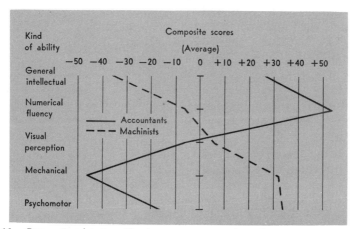

Figure 16. Occupational test profiles for accountants and machinists. *(From R. L. Thorndike and E. Hagen. 10,000 Careers. New York: John Wiley & Sons, Inc., 1959, pp. 27–28.)*

65

Factor Analysis

Another main line of development in the study of special abilities is an effort to discover what these abilities are by analyzing the *correlations* between test scores. We have referred to this in the previous chapter in discussing the evidence produced by Thurstone, Guilford, and others that what we measure as general intelligence can be broken down into more limited kinds of intellectual ability. As research progressed, it became apparent that what some psychologists were calling kinds of intelligence were the same characteristics that other psychologists had been calling vocational aptitudes. This has resulted in the construction of test batteries that are based on factor analysis but related to occupational criteria.

Factor analysis is a technique for analyzing tables of correlations between test scores so as to illuminate what different tests have in common. Figure 17 illustrates the kind of reasoning involved. Let us suppose that we have given three tests to a large group of high school students. By methods outlined in a previous chapter, we obtain three correlations between scores—for Tests A and B, Tests A and C, and Tests B and C. It turns out that all are positive, but the correlation between B and C is somewhat lower than the other two. How might we account for this situation? Usually, we assume that there are overlaps in the abilities measured by the three tests and that the correlations reveal how great these overlaps are. The shaded areas in Figure 17 constitute one way of showing this. It is the abilities represented by these areas, abilities which affect one's performance in more than one test, that the factor analyst seeks to locate. The situation with which the analyst actually works is usually a great deal more complicated than that shown in Figure 17. We are more likely to start with fifty tests than with three, and consider simultaneously the 1225 correlation coefficients obtained from them—(50 × 49) ÷ 2. After we find out which tests have something in common, we give their common "factor" a name based on our analysis of the reasoning, background experience, or special skill that seems to be involved in all the overlapping tests that determine the factor.

In using tests constructed by factor-analytic methods, it is important not to attach too much "reality" to the special abilities they appear to measure. *Factors* are essentially just hypotheses about intercorrelations in a battery of tests. Often such hypotheses are very useful aids in thinking about people; but they need to be checked against other information before definite conclusions are drawn.

THE GENERAL APTITUDE TEST BATTERY (GATB)

The most comprehensive program combining research on occupational skills themselves with factor-analytic study of the correlations between aptitude tests scores was set in motion in the early 1940s by the United States Employment Service. The investigators took upon themselves the task of identifying abilities essential to various kinds of occupations, constructing tests to measure these abilities, setting *minimum* scores on each of these tests. The General Aptitude Test Battery (GATB) is based on both *job* analysis leading to tests with predictive validity and *factor* analysis leading to tests of basic abilities. The nine aptitudes measured by this 2½ hour battery are G (general intelligence), V (verbal ability), N (numerical ability), S (spatial ability), P (form perception), Q (clerical perception), K (motor coordination), F (finger dexterity), and M (manual dexterity). Minimum scores in the critical aptitudes for each particular kind of occupation have been set. Fortunately, the same pattern of essential aptitudes often characterizes a number of related jobs, so the task of interpretation is not unwieldy. With the GATB, any employment

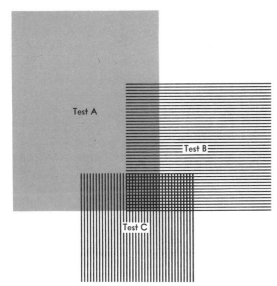

Test A

Test B

Test C

Figure 17. Relationships between what is measured by different tests as postulated by theory underlying factor analysis.

counselor can compare an individual's profile with each of thirty-six Occupational Ability Patterns that have been identified through research. These thirty-six basic patterns cover several hundred jobs. Thus, Don Dorf who takes the GATB may be made aware of many fields he has never considered, but for which he might qualify. He will also find out if he has less than the minimum amount of some special ability that seems to be required in a type of work he has been considering. For Don thinking about his future, this is a good return on the investment of about 2½ hours of testing time. The GATB shows what can be done when all the knowledge we have accumulated over the years about special vocational aptitudes is brought to bear on one practical problem. Much validity evidence still needs to be collected, however, and the conclusions about a person must be cautious ones. Like all aptitude tests, these are far from infallible.

Cautions in the use of Aptitude Tests

Our present thinking about the nature of special aptitudes and talents and about the techniques of constructing tests to measure them projects from both these lines of research—practical prediction studies and theoretical breakdowns of general intelligence by means of factor analysis. Published tests that have grown out of both branches of research are available for use in schools, personnel offices, and counseling services. It has become increasingly apparent, however, that we must be wary in making inferences from such tests. In screening applicants for a job or training program, it is usually necessary to try out the tests we propose to use in the specific situation, as correlations between tests and criteria vary widely from place to place. In using aptitude tests to help persons make vocational decisions, too, it is important to use tests that have been tried out in some practical situation so that that their relationship to real-life criteria is known. Special-ability tests based solely on factor analysis of correlations between tests do not tell us what we need to know about the way we are likely to perform in a criterion situation. Thus they may lead to unwise decisions.

Still another possible pitfall in the use of aptitude tests has become apparent as a result of efforts to place "disadvantaged" persons in productive employment. A test may be biased against groups with atypical backgrounds, so that it does not make valid predictions about how successful the members of these groups will be in occupations or training programs. To find out whether a particular test is or is not biased in this way requires a special research investigation of the problem. As emphasized in Chapter 3, *fairness* is becoming one of the fundamental standards by which tests for any particular purpose are evaluated.

SPECIAL CHARACTERISTICS
AND USES OF ACHIEVEMENT TESTS

Let us look now at some of the facts and principles we need to keep in mind when we use special-ability tests designed to measure achievement—what a person has learned or accomplished.

Essentially, a standardized school achievement test is only a refinement of the examination a teacher gives at the end of a course. Such tests are designed to do accurately and on a large scale what every teacher does routinely to find out how much of the material of a course each student has mastered. It is no accident that achievement tests have become big business in the United States. Our system of universal public education, secondary as well as primary, brings teachers and school administrators into contact with students drawn from an extremely wide range of home and community backgrounds. Yet because our schools are locally controlled, we have no standard curriculum for the country as a whole, and schools in some areas are far more effective than those elsewhere. Because Americans change residences frequently, children are constantly being shifted from one school system to another. Plainly, some standard way to find out how much an individual child knows about a given school subject is virtually a necessity of we are to make our educational system work. Educational achievement tests, therefore, meet a real social need.

Many of the research procedures we have already discussed were used in the production of such batteries of achievement tests as the Iowa Tests of Educational Development (ITED), the Sequential Tests of Educational Progress (STEP), the College Entrance Examination Board tests (CEEB), the American College Test (ACT), and the Graduate Record Examination (GRE). But the task of building these tests has some distinctive features. Chief among them is an emphasis on delineating the class of knowledge to be tested *before* starting to construct the test. This is not as easy as it might appear to be at first glance. If you were responsible, for example, for decisions about what should go into the American history test for high school students mentioned earlier, you would find yourself facing some difficult questions. Should the test be made up of factual questions about names, places, and dates? These are easiest to write and to score, but most history teachers do not consider the transmission of such factual knowledge the main purpose of their courses. Should one instead ask questions about historical movements and trends? If so, *which* movements, *which* trends? Historians differ in the emphasis they place on political, economic, and cultural movements; so do textbooks and teachers. Then should an American history test measure the *skills* as well as the knowledge that courses in this subject try to cultivate? Shall we include questions that will enable us to judge how well a student can read and understand historical passages, or how sound the student's reasoning is when tracing the historical roots of present-day situations and problems?

As suggested before, the most satisfactory way of handling this first step in the construction of an educational achievement test is to set up a committee of competent teachers to discuss the problems and come to some conclusions about what is to be measured. Even though such experts may disagree on details, they can usually reach an agreement about what materials and course objectives are really *basic*. It is this core of fundamental knowledge and skill around which the test should be constructed in order to be appropriate for many classrooms, many schools.

Once this core has been defined and a working outline derived from it, the next major task is to write test items that will be clear, fair, and meaningful. Because the test will be taken by thousands of students whose papers are usually scored by machine, such items must have one and only one right answer. Furthermore, this answer must not be too easy or obvious if the test is really to serve its purpose of distinguishing among students at many levels of knowledge and proficiency. The writing of good items is an *art*. There are rules for what to do and what not to do, but the skill, like other kinds of writing skill, is not really analyzable.

However, once these items have been written and put together in a trial form, statistical techniques are available to help the test maker decide which ones should be included in the final versions. First the test maker arranges to have several hundred people of the age or class for which the test is intended take the trial form, and he tabulates their responses to each item. From these tabulations indexes of *difficulty* and *discrimination* are derived. As for the former, while it is usually desirable to have a mixture of difficult and easy items in a test, questions that are so easy that almost everybody gets the right answer or so difficult that almost nobody gets it serve no useful purpose. In the final form they are omitted. A discrimination index for an item shows whether students who can be considered to be good at the kind of thinking the test is designed to measure (because their overall score is high) are more successful with the item than poor students are. An item that does not discriminate in this way is dead weight in a test, and it too is eliminated. It is not uncommon in the course of item analysis of a multiple-choice test to discover that on one particular question good students are actually more likely to choose one of the *wrong* responses than poor students are. Sometimes this happens because they employ a more complex and subtle reasoning than the author of the test anticipated. Naturally, such items are also eliminated before questions are selected for the final form of the test.

Once a satisfactory set of items has been assembled, the rest of the steps in the construction of an achievement test are much like those discussed in Chapter 3. The test maker must explore reliability, and express it as a reliability coefficient, or standard error of measurement. The test maker must specify standardized procedures for administering and scoring the test, and must work out a meaningful derived score based on a representative sample of the population for which the test is intended. And norm tables must be prepared. As explained previously, if sound decisions about what is to go into the test have been made all along the line, *content* validity is insured.

We have been considering achievement tests from the *producer's* viewpoint. But what does the *consumer*—teacher, school administrator, or the testee—need to keep in mind in evaluating these tests and the scores obtained from them? There are so many achievement tests available for measuring what people know about nearly all school subjects at all educational levels that a choice is often difficult. The primary consideration is the one stressed in the preceding paragraphs—content validity. In deciding which of the available batteries of achievement test to use, for example, a school administrator examines the test and reads very carefully the section of the manual in which the authors explain how the basic outline was developed and how the questions were chosen. If the administrator finds this task has been done well, the test may be considered as a possibility. The administrator will then go on to evaluate its other characteristics—how reliable it is, how convenient it is to administer and score, what the norm groups are like. Perhaps what needs to be stressed most is that to judge the content validity of a test we must do more than examine the test questions themselves. What seems to be a question with a simple factual answer may call for a complex reasoning process. What seems to be an adequate assortment of questions on different principles and concepts may be quite overbalanced in one direction. *Content validity* rests on the whole set of procedures used in planning and constructing the test. *Face validity* alone—what one can judge simply from looking at the questions—is not an adequate basis for choosing a test.

COMBINATION APTITUDE-ACHIEVEMENT BATTERIES

Because there is no clear line separating achievement from aptitude tests, and because special-ability tests of all kinds have turned out to be helpful in schools and counseling offices, *combination* batteries have been worked out for use in educational situations. One group that has been widely used in high schools is called *Differential Aptitude Tests* (DAT). It is composed of eight separate tests: (1) Verbal Reasoning, (2) Numerical Ability, (3) Abstract Reasoning, (4) Space Reasoning, (5) Mechanical Reasoning, (6) Clerical Speed and Accuracy, (7) Spelling, and (8) Sentences. The abilities measured by some of these tests are influenced more by a student's school experience, while the abilities measured by others are affected more by out-of-school experience. The authors and publisher of the battery have collected a large body of information about what one can predict from a student's scores on these tests. Such predictions may not be so sharp and clear as we might wish—it is not at all certain, for example, that a boy with a high score in Numerical Ability will do better in mathematics courses than a classmate who is high in Verbal Reasoning. But by studying the information the publishers furnish with this test, a teacher or counselor can find out what predictions are possible and how definitely they can be stated. The advantage of a battery of tests of this sort over a single measure of general intelligence is that it is more likely to reveal for every student some assets that they can count on in planning for their futures. The advantage it has over a miscellaneous collection of aptitude and achievement tests is that the norms for all tests are based on the same representative group of people. Thus, the scores that show where an individual stands in relation to this norm population are comparable from test to test, and we can say with assurance, for example, that Hugh ranks much higher in mechanical reasoning than in verbal reasoning.

There are several others of this combination type, and more are likely to become available as time passes. As the search for innate abilities has been abandoned, another question has come into clear focus. What is *useful* to measure about a person in order to facilitate decisions about the person's future. In this vein, it is *useful* to understand what kind of special ability the individual possesses, regardless of how this ability was developed. The concept of *special ability*, which emphasizes what can be done with talents rather than where they came from, may gradually take the place of the *aptitude* and *achievement* concepts that have played so important a part in the development of testing methods in the past.

One research undertaking that is in progress right now should eventually throw a good deal of light on questions about how special abilities are used. It is called Project TALENT.[1] In the spring of 1960, 440,000 students in 1353 high schools spent two days taking tests. The tests in the TALENT battery had been carefully designed and pretested in order that they might tap as many abilities as possible; 37 separate scores were obtained for each subject. The schools in which testing was done were carefully selected to constitute a complete cross-section of secondary schools in the United States. Besides the test data, many kinds of information were collected about students, schools, and communities. The plan has been to follow up these testees in 1961, 1965, 1970, and 1980 to find out what has happened to them—the careers they chose, the education they obtained, their achievements and contributions to society. When the analysis of this formidable body of data is complete, it should tell us more than we have ever known before about what happens to people with different special talents under different circumstances. At each stage of the project, reports are being published to keep the public informed about what has been learned so far.

The development of special-ability testing has coincided with an increasing awareness by Americans that society as a whole benefits when individuals are encouraged to use their talents effectively

---

[1] Project TALENT, financed by the Department of Health, Education, and Welfare, is being conducted by the American Institutes for Research and the University of Pittsburgh.

and accomplish as much as they can. In this very real sense, what is good for one is good for the country. To the extent that they can help us achieve this joint individual-social purpose, such tests are worth the effort and ingenuity expended on them. Accordingly, they occupy an important position in the total structure of psychological measurement today.

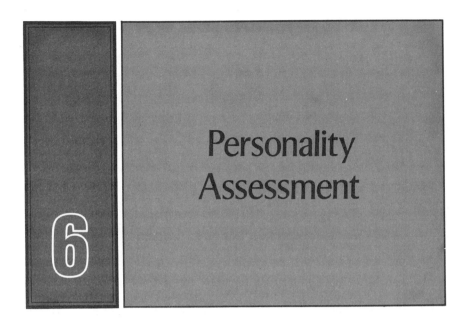

Personality
Assessment

As we look around us at the people we know, and as we examine our own lives, it is apparent that some of the most distinctive personal qualities cannot be classified as abilities at all. We usually do not know or need to know the score our next-door neighbor makes on a clerical test, but we do find ourselves making some necessary estimate of his friendliness, neatness, cooperativeness, generosity, dependability, and attitudes about politics. Such qualities are essential to the business of living, for success depends on them fully as much as it does on competence. And social problems such as crime and mental illness involve faulty personal habits in individuals rather than lack of ability. Clearly, as children grow from infancy to adulthood, emotional maturity is at least as important to development as intellectual maturity. Thus, it is not strange that psychologists should have taken up the challenge to measure personality traits as well as abilities.

SPECIAL DIFFICULTIES
AND WAYS OF OVERCOMING THEM

The measurement of personality characteristics involves some special problems in addition to those posed by the measurement of abilities. The most troublesome of these, and the one that constitutes the major difference between ability and personality tests, is that the strategy of placing a testee in a standard situation and obtaining an actual *sample* of behavior is not feasible. We simply cannot set up in the testing room the standard situations in which personality traits are most likely to manifest themselves. Many of the most important of these traits are *social* in nature and show up only when an individual finds himself in a certain kind of group. In order really to sample such a trait as self-control, for instance, we would have to standardize situations that were irritating, frustrating, annoying. (Military psychologists tried to do this during World War II by making insulting remarks to persons who were attempting to concentrate on complex psychomotor tasks, but their efforts were not successful. Being insulted by a mental tester is not the same as being insulted by one's superior officer, even though the two situations may look alike.) In ability testing, the use of sample situations is feasible. Problems posed in the testing room can be similar in most essential respects to the problems a person encounters in special situations in life. But in testing personality it is difficult to reproduce the *social* situations in which personality chiefly manifests itself. There has been some challenging research in which this was attempted, but so far no generally usable tests have emerged from it.

Personality testers have adopted two kinds of strategy to enable them to get around this difficulty. The first is to substitute *reported* behavior for *observed* behavior. This has produced the many personality questionnaires and inventories we find in frequent use today. The second is to present an ambiguous stimulus such as an inkblot or a picture and ask the testee to react to it, on the assumption that one's response must necessarily reflect a personal style and orientation. We shall consider each of these approaches separately.

PERSONALITY INVENTORIES

In following the first of these approaches, substituting reported for observed behavior, the test-maker first thinks of some questions or statements that represent various manifestations of the trait to be measured. Suppose, for example, this is *self-control*. The test maker may think of ten questions having to do with holding one's temper under provocation. The assumption is made that the person who says yes to nine of them has more self-control than a person who says yes to only five.

This method of testing personality was invented at about the same time as group intelligence tests were. During World War I, Robert S. Woodworth put together a set of questions similar to those psychiatrists ask in screening recruits for emotional stability. This first collection of questions, called the Personal Data Sheet, was the progenitor of a long line of subsequent tests of general adjustment, neuroticism, and other traits related to mental illness and health.

This method—asking a testee to answer questions about his or her behavior and feelings in life situations—carries with it some testing problems unlike those encountered in ability measurement. The history of personality testing, indeed, can be viewed as a series of efforts to solve these special problems. The most obvious, though perhaps not the most serious, snag is that a person may not tell the truth. In measuring abilities we do not have to worry about this. It is not likely that a boy with an IQ of 90 will be able to "fake" an IQ of 120. Unless his mind works at the 120 level, he is not able to answer the questions so as to attain that score. But it is quite possible for a fearful person to give "brave" answers to questions about reactions to danger, or for a withdrawn person to say yes to the question, "Do you have many friends?" If a person's suitability for a job, a college, or an exclusive club is to be judged on the basis of personality test scores, that individual is under a real temptation to fake.

Military psychologists also found out that at times a person may be tempted to "fake bad." Some draftees who showed what looked like serious psychiatric disabilities on the initial screening test were adjudged quite healthy when more penetrating methods of examining them were employed. They had hoped to be classified neurotic and answered the questions toward that end.

Psychologists have been quite ingenious about devising ways of discovering whether answers have been faked, so that a score can be either discarded or corrected for deception. Their technique is to include in the inventory answers that sound attractive to a person who wishes to produce a "good" score (or sound seriously maladjusted to a person trying to produce a "bad" score) but which experience has shown are very seldom chosen by respondents giving honest answers. The larger the number of these particular responses a person gives, the greater is the likelihood that the individual is faking.

This does not solve the whole problem of obtaining a true report, however. A person is often *unable* to describe personal motives and emotional characteristics honestly even when wishing and intending to do so. As Freud made us aware, a large part of our motivation is unconscious, and the pull of unconscious wishes distorts our view of our own personalities. The man with strong dependent needs often sees himself as an aggressive, self-reliant individualist. The woman with a powerful current of hostility in her relations with her family may see herself as gentle and self-sacrificing. Thus, any score may not mean what it seems to mean.

Furthermore, scores may be partially determined by *response sets* of various kinds. One of these is *social desirability*, the tendency to choose responses that reflect what is considered to be the "right" way of behaving and feeling in our society. Another is *acquiescence*, the tendency to agree with what someone else says, to answer yes rather than no. While research has shown that response sets do not generally affect personality test scores as much as was feared, one must always be on the lookout for them in individual cases.

An additional complication in attempting to assess personality characteristics by asking people questions about themselves has become increasingly apparent. In these days of sophisticated systems for the storage and retrieval of data, many people have become apprehensive about possible consequences to themselves at some later time of the answers they give to questions about "sensitive" matters such as sex, religion, or politics. The individual's right to privacy must be taken seriously by the makers and users of personality tests. A person should not be asked to take a personality test without a good personal or scientific reason, and arrangements for safeguarding the confidentiality or anonymity of the records should be built into the original testing plan. Procedures for accomplishing this are available. Their utilization is an ethical responsibility of the person who gives personality tests.

Another, rather different, difficulty psychologists have run into in devising personality tests has been the lack of unambiguous criteria for evaluating test validity. As we have seen, one standard method for validating ability tests is to correlate test scores with nontest indicators of the trait measured. The tradition began with intelligence tests. Binet took it for granted that the trait he was trying to measure was the same as the trait teachers observed in their bright, average, and dull students. Thus, he could find out whether his tests were measuring this characteristic by correlating test scores with teacher judgments, as expressed in school marks, promotions, and the like.

In the case of most of the personality qualities we might wish to measure, however, it is difficult to obtain criterion measures from life. We can, of course, ask people to rate their students, employees, fraternity brothers, or neighbors for optimism, dependability, or general adjustment. But such ratings are unsatisfactory in many ways as measures of personality. First, raters often disagree markedly in their evaluation of the same person, reflecting their own attitudes perhaps as much as the characteristics of the person they are rating. Second, ratings show what is usually called a "halo" effect—that is, a person who elicits generally favorable attitudes tends to receive high ratings on everything; a person not generally liked is rated low on everything. Furthermore, it is difficult to persuade raters to spread their judgments over a range of numbers; if the rating scale runs from 1 to 9, they hesitate to give anyone a 1 or a 9 and may rate everybody 5, 6, or 7. Had ratings been more satisfactory as a way of measuring personality, perhaps there would not have been as much pressure to develop personality tests themselves. However, ratings are still widely used, both for evaluating personality in practical situations and for exploring the relationships of personality tests to other measures. One does not discard a dull tool until a sharper one is available! But in interpreting ratings we must always take their deficiencies into consideration. They are not really satisfactory criteria for personality tests.

One way of investigating the validity of personality tests is to compare defined groups of people singled out by society on the basis of some trait. This method has been particularly useful in research on neurotic and psychotic tendencies, for the extremely maladjusted are likely to show up eventually for psychiatric treatment. Assuming that there is an underlying continuum of adjustment and that psychiatric patients as a group represent one end of it, then evidence that they obtain extreme scores on an adjustment inventory becomes evidence for the validity of the test. (This is an oversimplification. There are several *kinds* of maladjustment represented by groups with different psychiatric diagnoses, so that not one but a number of traits must be assumed. But the same reasoning applies to the complex situation.)

The availability of clearly defined groups to facilitate the validation of adjustment–maladjustment tests has stimulated research in this particular area, as has the demand for tests in mental hospitals and clinics. This concentration of research efforts has resulted in many more tests for *negative* than for *positive* personality traits. It is much easier to discover, for example, that Lawrence Wylie has a strong undercurrent of anxiety, a tendency toward paranoid thinking, and more than the usual number of psychosomatic symptoms than it is to assess his dependability, loyalty, and leadership potential. We must keep in mind this negative bias of personality measurement whenever we use personality tests.

To some extent, this negative bias is being corrected as research continues. In one area, the measurement of vocational interests, E. K. Strong was able to capitalize on the existence of occupational groups in constructing the Strong Vocational Interest Blank, a valuable test for measuring motivations that determine life decisions. In another large research program, David C. McClelland and others tackled the *achievement motive* and devised ways of measuring it. We shall have more to say about these particular tests later. Here they serve only as examples of a trend in research that will eventually round out the field of personality measurement so that we can assess favorable traits as adequately as unfavorable traits.

As research with personality inventories has continued over the years, progress in several directions has been made. First of all, instead of being simply a catalog of miscellaneous symptoms, as the earliest "adjustment" inventories tended to be, an instrument is now designed to provide several scores on separate traits. The well-known Minnesota Multiphasic Personality Inventory (MMPI), for example, started out with nine scales through which different varieties of psychiatric difficulty could be identified. Many others have been added as timed passed—scales to measure such nonpsychiatric variables as social introversion. The Edwards Personal Preference Schedule measures fifteen kinds of personality *needs*, such as need for order, need for affiliation, and the like.

One of the principal ways in which multiple scoring keys for the same set of test items have been constructed is through *item analysis*. This involves the tabulation of answers actually given to the questions by members of groups specially selected to represent the personality tendency one wishes to measure. Responses on which a clear, statistically significant difference shows up between this group and a group representing the general population constitute the scoring key for this personality characteristic. On the MMPI referred to above, for example, a response is scored on the scale for Paranoia only if it is one which paranoid patients give more frequently than normal patients do. This procedure is called the *empirical* method of personality test development—meaning that *experience* rather than theory or common sense determines what responses should be counted toward each score.

The availability of this empirical technique for constructing scoring keys has led to another significant trend in personality testing. It has become apparent that in many situations a *tailor-made* instrument, produced especially for a particular research project or a particular selection situation, usually works better than a standardized test designed to measure general personality traits. For example, researchers had very little success in identifying motivational variables related to underachievement in school until they followed the procedure sketched above—actually comparing, item by item, the responses of groups of good and poor students.

Another principal way in which multiple scoring keys for a comprehensive set of personality items have been produced is through *factor analysis.* To proceed in this way, one first asks a large group of subjects, as representative as possible of the population for which the test is being designed, to respond to the items. The next step is to correlate responses to every item with responses to every other item, thus producing a huge table of intercorrelations. By the procedures explained in the previous chapter, factor analysis translates these intercorrelations into factors that can be labeled or named by inspecting the pattern of factor loadings. Raymond B. Cattell has been the leading proponent of this method of producing comprehensive personality tests.

As examples of what has been accomplished in the field of personality measurement, let us look now at a few widely used inventories: the Strong Vocational Interest Blank (SVIB); the Strong-Campbell Interest Inventory (SCII)—the latest edition of the Strong Vocational Interest Blank; the Self Directed Search (SDS); the Kuder Occupational Interest Survey (KOIS); the California Psychological Inventory (CPI); and the Minnesota Multiphasic Personality Inventory (MMPI).

The Strong Vocational Interest Blank is an empirically scored instrument with a long and distinguished history. Soon after World War I, E. K. Strong, Jr. and some other psychologists happened upon an interesting fact—that different groups of professional people showed consistent differences in what they said they liked and disliked. Some of these differences were what common sense would have predicted. It is natural that more engineers than salesmen should say that they like physics, for example. But significant differences also turned up on items having no apparent connection with jobs—items concerned with amusements, hobbies, people, books, and many other aspects of life. Such findings suggested that a profession may represent a way of life as well as a way of earning a living. Strong saw that it would be possible to measure these characteristics that are related to occupational choice. In a systematic program of research extending over many years, he worked with men from one occupational group after another, comparing the responses they gave to the test questions with the responses given by men in general. In constructing a scoring key for the Architect scale, for example, he asked several hundred practicing architects to take the test. Item by item, he tabulated their answers to find out which ones they answered "Like," which "Indifferent," and which "Dislike." Any answer for which the difference between architects and men in general was statistically significant was included in the Architect scoring key. Later, Strong devised a special form of the test for women, and developed scales for "women's" occupations in the same way. Norms for all the occupational groups studied were provided, and the relationship of interest scores to age, special abilities, and many other human characteristics were explored.

The SCII, Strong-Campbell Interest Inventory (Campbell, 1977)—the most recent edition of the SVIB, was published in 1974. The publication of the SCII was marked by at least two major changes: the men's and women's test booklets were merged into a single form, and a theoretical framework was introduced to structure the profile and the interpretation of the scores. The combining of the men's and women's forms into one booklet, answer sheet, and profile was based on the notion of equal treatment for both men and women. Items that appeared to have a sexual bias were eliminated, and references to gender (e.g., "policeman") were changed. The current form of the SCII permits men and women to be scored on all existing scales of the inventory. This has been brought about by scoring against same-sex people, opposite-sex people, and on a combined-sex sample.

A theoretical framework for the SCII germinated from John Holland's theory of personality types and environmental models. (Holland's theory is discussed more specifically in chapter 7.) Holland (1973) believes that interests are an expression of personality and that people tend to resemble one or more personality types (Realistic, Investigative, Artistic, Social, Enterprising, and Conventional). These types have been defined by Holland by means of the Vocational Preference Inventory (Holland, 1975) and the Self Directed Search (1972). The coupling of Holland's theory and Strong's empirical work was stimulated by the fact that Holland's six personality types were found to resemble the dimensions frequently appearing in research with the SVIB scales. Based on this evidence, David Campbell became convinced that Holland's personality types were useful for organizing, understanding, and interpreting the scales of the SVIB. Campbell's notion and some follow-up research revealed that the Holland types could be used with SVIB items and archival data in a meaningful way for men and women. These findings led to the use of Holland's theory and personality types for organizing the profile of the SCII.

In its present form, the SCII consists of 325 items drawn from several areas of life—occupations, school subjects, activities, amusements, types of people, activity preferences, and personal characteristics. Scoring agencies routinely report scores for six general occupational themes (Realistic, Investigative, Artistic, Social, Enterprising, and Conventional), for 23 basic-interest scales, 124 occupational scales, two special scales, and nine administrative indexes. The six general-theme scores reported suggest a global view of the individual's occupational orientation—the general kinds of activities enjoyed, the type of occupational environment liked, general coping style, and the kind of people a person tends to get along with. The six themes are briefly described below:

Realistic—outdoor and technical interests
Investigative—scientific and inquiring interests
Artistic—dramatic and self-expressive interests
Social—helping and people-oriented interests
Enterprising—persuasive, political, and power-oriented interests
Conventional—organized and clerical interests

The basic-interest scales measure interests in particular kinds of activity such as science, mechanical activities, and athletics. High scores mean strong interest and liking for activities in the area. The occupational scales couple the individual's pattern of interests with the working world by telling the person how his or her interests (likes and dislikes) resemble those of experienced workers happily employed in a variety of different occupations. The special scales (the academic-orientation scale and the introversion-extroversion scale) were previously called the nonoccupational scales. The academic-orientation scale indicates degree of academic orientation (e.g., people who are highly educated or are motivated to become so). The introversion-extroversion scale suggests the person's interest in being alone as opposed to working with other people.

The administration indexes are checks on each answer sheet to make sure that errors have not occurred in the administration, completion, or processing of the answer sheet. The meaning of the scores is explained on the back of the profile sheet the testee receives, and more completely in the interpretion manual. The second edition of the manual (Campbell, 1977) has a new chapter on interpretation which includes an outline of a counseling procedure and a number of detailed case studies. Figures 18 and 19 show what an individual's profile looks like, and an illustrative case.

On the basis of extensive research extending over more than four decades, we know a number of things about vocational interests as measured by the Strong blank. First, patterns of likes and dislikes are not primarily the result of participation in an occupation, but exist *before* a person enters it. For example, Stanford students who were later to enter medical school and become physicians, scored high on Strong's *Physician* scale even in their undergraduate days. Most people, it seems, develop their individual interest patterns before they leave high school.

Second, for most persons, once such interest patterns are set they are as stable and permanent as any aspect of personality that has been studied. Strong kept in touch with many of the Stanford

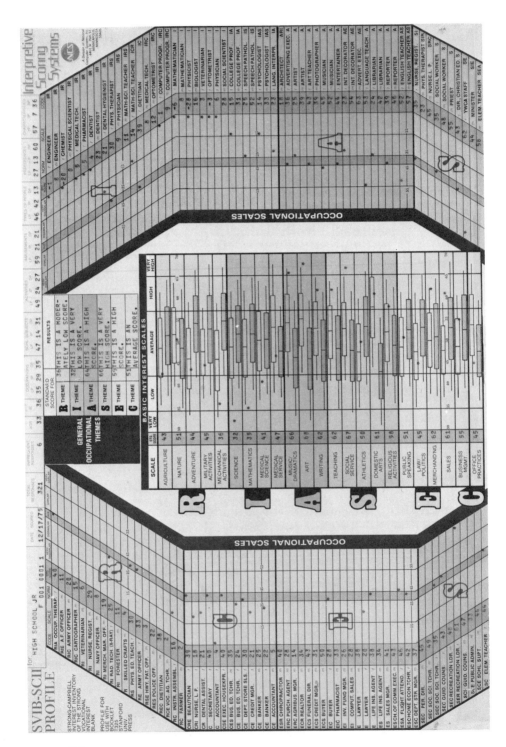

84

GENERAL OCCUPATIONAL
THEMES

R   47   Moderately low
I   47   Average
A   36   Moderately low
S   46   Average
E   62   Moderately high
C   41   Moderately low

(E)

HIGH BASIC INTEREST SCALES

R   Military Activities   73
E   Sales   70
R   Adventure   63
R   Nature   61
E   Merchandising   61
R   Agriculture   58

(RE)

LOW BASIC INTEREST SCALES

A   Writing   30
A   Art   37
S   Religious Activities   37
I   Science   39
S   Social Service   39
C   Office Practices   40
A   Music/Dramatics   41

FIVE HIGHEST
OCCUPATIONAL SCALES

SEC   Personnel Director   53
 EI   Investment Fund Manager   52
ECR   Realtor   51
 ES   Life Insurance Agent   49
 ES   Sales Manager   49

FIVE LOWEST
OCCUPATIONAL SCALES

  A   Librarian   −4
 IR   Physical Scientist   −1
IRC   Medical Technologist   4
IAS   Psychologist   8
  A   Artist   9

(ES)

(E)

Academic Orientation   32
Introversion-Extroversion   43
Percentage Yes: Characterisics 50

Figure 19. Summary of scores for case A from the Strong-Campbell Interest Inventory. *Source: D. P. Campbell, Manual for the SVIB-SCII Strong-Campbell Interest Inventory (2nd edition). Stanford, California: Stanford University Press, 1977. Copyright 1977 by Stanford University Press, and reproduced with permission. This is a summary of scores on the SCII for an outgoing, sales-oriented, realistic person with a strong liking for risk taking and making money.*

Comments for the Counselor on Interpreting the SCII

The Strong-Campbell Interest Inventory is a revision and extension of the widely used Strong Vocational Interest Blank. The SCII can be used with anyone who understands the vocabulary of the test items, that is, most people over 16. The inventory can be used for special projects as early as the eighth grade (age 14), but although profiles for students of 14 or 15 do reflect their current interests, they may not accurately predict future interests or careers. At this age, the inventory should be used mainly as a vehicle for discussion of the world of work. By age 17, definite patterns emerge that remain fairly stable, and by age 25, most people's interests are well established.

The profile reflects the patterns of answers made to the inventory, patterns that can be related statistically to the interests of men and women in particular occupations, and the results can best be used as general predictions of where the individual can find occupational satisfaction. The best help a counselor can give is to help students realize the importance of the overall patterns in their scores. Most students tend to overemphasize the importance of one or two high (or low) scores that may, for various reasons, be misleading. The emphasis should be on long-term development rather than on making immediate decisions. Students often need help in finding more information about the areas where they scored high, and they usually need to be reminded that this is a test of interests, not aptitudes.

An individual's scores on this inventory are determined by the responses that he or she made to the inventory, and these responses are based on that person's perception of what he or she likes and dislikes, perceptions that are developed from a variety of experiences and attitudes. Because one of the purposes of this inventory is to call the person's attention to occupational areas that he or she might enjoy but had not considered previously, counselors should be especially alert to situations where a person is ignoring an occupation that looks appropriate from the profile pattern simply because he or she has had no exposure to that occupation. This means, for example, that when a young woman scores high in the medical science/medical service area, and is considering nursing as a career, she should also be encouraged to consider other possibilities, such as medical or dental school. In general, the inventory should be used to help people focus on such special areas of interests and, within these areas, to look at the broadest possible hierarchy of occupations. In the past, some people have restricted their career options because of real or imagined barriers to their entry into certain occupations, especially racial, sexual, or age barriers. Such barriers are now falling, and virtually all occupations are now legally open to all qualified persons; consequently, students and others completing this inventory should give serious consideration to *all* occupations falling within their indicated sphere of interest.

Men and women, even those in the same occupation, give somewhat different responses to the inventory. As the norms for the Basic Interest Scales demonstrate, these differences are most prominent in the artistic and domestic areas, which tend to be favored by women, and in the mechanical area, favored by men. To have ignored the various sex-linked differences in the norming of the Occupational Scales would have introduced significant error. Until men's interests no longer differ notably from women's, separate scales will provide more meaningful results. And because some occupations continue to be dominated by one sex—"farmer," for example, or "secretary"—Occupational Scales have not yet been developed for both sexes in all cases. Research is under way toward reconciling these disparities of the real world with the purposes of interest inventories.

On the reverse side of the student's copy of the profile is a basic explanation of the three principal classes of scales; with the help of these comments, most students can understand their own scores. The counselor can help, first, by explaining the finer technical details; second, by explaining any apparent inconsistencies between scores of different types; and third, by helping students integrate this information with such data as are available on their aptitudes and experiences.

The General Occupational Themes

These six themes, described briefly on the student's copy of the profile, are based on J. L. Holland's work, *Making Vocational Choices: A Theory of Careers* (Prentice-Hall, 1973). His book

is an excellent source for further information about these themes and the world of work.

Holland's chief premise is that each of us can be described in terms of relative similarity to one or more of six idealized occupational-interest personality types, and that each type seeks out a different kind of occupational environment. Thus, personality types do as much as job requirements to establish the working tenor of a given occupation. Although this formulation is oversimplified, it offers a useful structure—one that conforms to empirical research results—for analyzing the differences between people and the occupations they choose. Most important, Holland's theory offers an organizing structure for the extensive network of empirical studies carried out over the years with the Strong inventories.

The six themes or scales each contain 20 items, scored positively for "Like" responses and negatively for "Dislike" responses. Norms have been established by scoring a general sample of 600 people (300 men and 300 women), then assigning this sample a mean of 50 and a standard deviation of 10, as a basis for converting future raw scores to standard scores. The numerical score, printed out under "Std Score," is based on this combined norm sample. Because males and females score somewhat differently on these scales, printed interpretive comments—"This is a HIGH score" and so forth—are supplied; these comments are based on comparisons with people of the same sex as the person being tested (and for this reason the correct sex must be indicated on the answer sheet). In some cases, therefore, men and women with the same numerical score will be furnished different printed comments. Within each sex, the interpretive comments correspond to the following percentile ranges:

Very high	94th and above
High	85th–93rd
Moderately high	70th–84th
Average	31st–69th
Moderately low	16th–30th
Low	7th–15th
Very low	6th and below

The six themes can be arranged in the form of a hexagon, as shown on the student's copy of the profile, in such a way that themes falling next to each other (that is, on adjacent corners) are the most similar to each other, and those directly across the hexagon from each other are the most dissimilar. These similarities and differences among extreme types are useful in interpreting the student's scores.

The General Themes should be used to help the student identify a general section of the occupational world for more intensive study. The two or three themes where the student has scored highest should be noted, and then (in conjunction with results on the Basic Interest Scales) compared with the occupations listed in the Occupational Scales section that relate strongly to the same themes. Conjunctions of high scores on particular Occupational Scales *and* on their related General Theme and Basic Interest Scales are particularly worth noting.

The descriptions of the extreme types for the six themes, given on the student's copy of the profile, have been carefully worded to avoid unfavorable connotations or the appearance of valuations. Still, people might occasionally resent these characterizations, particularly in a nonpsychiatric instrument. But what seems to happen is that a person scoring high on a particular theme feels gratified by being thus described and tends to look coolly upon the other, dissimilar types; whereas someone scoring moderately on all six themes reads nothing particularly into any of the descriptions.

The Basic Interest Scales

The Basic Interest Scales are homogeneous scales; they were constructed by clustering together items with high intercorrelations. Because the item content is closely focused on only the single topic indicated by the scale name, the scales are relatively easy to understand. "Like" responses to these items are scored positively, "Dislike" responses negatively; thus the level of scores is somewhat related to the percentage of "Like" and "Dislike" responses given. People who give many "Like" responses, say 50 percent or more, will have many more high scores here than those who give only a few, say 15 percent or fewer. For this reason, the LP and DP indexes, described below under "Administrative Indexes," will be useful in interpreting these scales. (These comments apply also to the General Occupational Themes.)

The Basic Interest Scales have been normed on a general sample of 600 men and women; the combined sample has been assigned a standard-score mean of 50 and standard deviation of 10 on each scale. Norms for the two sexes are indicated by the bars printed on the scales; the shaded bar gives the norm for men, the open bar the norm for women. The thick portion of the bar defines the middle half of the sample, from the 25th to the 75th percentile; the thin, extending lines run from the 10th to the 90th percentile; and the vertical line indicates the mean.

The Basic Interest Scales have been arranged in clusters corresponding to their relationships to the General Occupational Themes. Usually there is a marked consistency in the patterns of scores on the two scale types. For example, a person who scores high on the REALISTIC theme will have at least some high scores in the corresponding cluster of Basic Interest Scales.

Workers in occupations directly related to a given scale score 8–10 points higher on that scale than the general sample does; that is, salespeople average about 60 on the SALES scale, scientists about 60 on the SCIENCE scale, artists about 60 on the ART scale, and so forth. Thus, scores over 60 should be considered high; on those few scales showing substantial sex differences, scores 10 points above the relevant sex mean are high.

Scores on the Basic Interest Scales do not change much with age, though there is a tendency for scores to creep upward slightly, perhaps 3 or 4 points on the average, between the teenage years and adulthood. One major exception is the ADVENTURE scale, on which teenage boys score about 8–10 points *higher* than adults. Scores on ATHLETICS and MILITARY ACTIVITIES also tend to decrease slightly with age.

The Occupational Scales

Each Occupational Scale was developed by testing 200–300 happily employed men or women (depending on the scale) in that occupation, then isolating the items that they answered differently from the general sample; these items then became the scale for that sex working in that occupation. The scales have been normed by setting the mean of the occupational sample equal to 50, the standard deviation to 10. Thus, a student scoring 50 on a given scale has responded to these characteristic items in the same way the average member of that occupation does. A student scoring in the "average" range—between 26 and 44— has responded to these items the way people-in-general do. Since scores in this range are of little value in profiling the student's interests, they are not discriminated in the profile plotting (the screened area accommodates two asterisk positions—one for scores from 26 to 35, the other for scores from 36 to 44).

Each of the occupations has been given a code type corresponding to its high General Theme scores; the code types are indicated on the profile, and have been used to order the scales. Students should be encouraged to note that the code types of the Occupational Scales where they have high scores usually correspond to their high scores on the General Themes.

The Occupational Scales are more complex than either of the other two types of scales: they include more items; they include items with a wider variety of content; and they score some "Dislike" responses positively (for example, if the members of an occupation dislike an activity substantially more than the general population does, the "Dislike" response to that activity will be weighted positively). Thus, a person can score high on an Occupational Scale by sharing patterns of aversions with the members of that occupation, as well as by sharing their "Likes."

The Occupational Scales should not be seen as precise predictors of occupations where the student will be happy, but only as suggestions. High scores should also be used as leads to related occupations that are not on the profile. And the student should be especially cautioned to infer not that "I scored high on the FARMER scale, therefore I'd be a good farmer," but rather that "I have answered the inventory in much the way farmers do."

Following each Occupational Scale is an "f" or "m" indicating the sex of the sample used to establish the scale. Although same-sex scales are more valid for the individual than other-sex scales, everyone is scored on all scales, to ensure that maximum information is made available to everyone. But only the scores for the same-sex scales, which merit more attention, are plotted visually.

The Administrative Indexes

These indexes are checks to make certain that the answer sheet was completed and processed correctly. The first one, TOTAL RESPONSES, shows how many answer marks the computer has read from the answer sheet; since there are 325 items, the score on this index should be 325 or close to it. Up to 20 items can be omitted without significantly affecting the results.

The second index, INFREQUENT RESPONSES, shows the number of rare responses given. It is weighted so that almost everyone scores zero or higher here; if the score is below zero, the person has marked an uncommonly high number of rare responses (this weighting technique permits the counselor simply to ignore this index, unless it is negative). Usually a negative score indicates some confusion, such as skipping a number on the answer sheet, or random marking.

The remaining indexes show the percentage of "Like" (LP) "Indifferent" (IP), and "Dislike" (DP) responses made to th various sections of the inventory. These percentages can be qui useful in detecting problems—for example, if a section was l blank on the answer sheet the percentages for it will be 0-0- The percentages can also be useful in identifying unusual r sponse patterns. Because the General Themes and Basic Intere Scales are scored positively for "Like" responses and negative for "Dislike" responses, when the percentage of "Like" or "Di like" responses varies greatly from the usual split of rough 33-33-33, say to 90-8-2, the level of scores on these scales w: be affected. But although these percentages are useful in unde standing the student's response style, they should not be ove interpreted; some people produce extreme percentages, yet sti have a "normal" pattern on the profile. The tolerance of th scoring system for extreme test-taking strategies is considerabl The distributions of these percentages for a general sample (men and women are given in the *Manual*.

The Special Scales

The AOR (ACADEMIC ORIENTATION) scale contains items th discriminate between students who do well in academic setting and those who do not, and as such can be considered an "O(cupational Scale" for "college student." Students graduating wit a B.A. from a liberal arts college average about 50, M.A.s abou 55, Ph.D.s about 60. Most students gain about 10 points on th scale over their 4 years of college; thus, the scores of freshme should be judged with that in mind. The item content is heavil oriented toward science and the arts (weighted positively) an business and blue-collar activities (weighted negatively).

On the IE (INTROVERSION-EXTROVERSION) scale, high score (60 and above) indicate introversion and low scores (40 and be low), extroversion. The item content is concerned almost entirel with working with people in social service, educational, entertain ment, or business settings.

Males and females score about the same, on both scales.

Inconsistencies Between Scales

There are three main types of scores on the profile, and one o: the tasks of the counselor is to straighten out misunderstand ings about the differences.

The three types of scores can be better understood by usin; an analogy to descriptions of physical build. The General Occu pational Themes are concerned with global categories, and are similar to such overall descriptions as "She is tall and slender" o "He is small and wiry." The Basic Interest Scales are concerned with specific attributes and are similar to statements such as "She weighs 118 pounds" or "He has a reach of 38 inches." The Oc cupational Scales are concerned with how the person resembles other types of people, and are analogous to statements such as "She has the build of a swimmer" or "He looks like a jockey." Thus, although the three types of scales report three types of scores, a general thread of consistency runs through all of them.

One kind of confusion arises when the score on a specific Basic Interest Scale—such as ART or AGRICULTURE—is high and the score on the related Occupational Scale—ARTIST or FARMER—is low. This happens because the Occupational Scales are more complex in content than the Basic Interest Scales; they contain *all* of the substantial differences between the people in those occupations and people in general. The FARMER scale, for example, contains items involving mechanical activities as well as agriculture, and also items involving rejection of social service, artistic, and leadership pursuits. To score high, one must resemble farmers in many of these areas, and not simply share their agricultural interests.

Inconsistencies like this can be useful in counseling. A student who questions an apparent inconsistency between a high score on the AGRICULTURE Basic Scale and a low score on the FARMER scale is usually receptive to a discussion of the "environment" of an occupation; that is, that to be satisfied with farming as a career involves more than simply liking agriculture. Farming involves a way of life, working with machines and animals and not so much with people; it is physically demanding; and for many "intellectual types" it has little appeal. Other inconsistencies—between, say, ART and ARTIST, MATHEMATICS and MATHEMATICIAN, or MILITARY ACTIVITIES and ARMY OFFICER—can lead to equally fruitful discussions.

Further Information

The SVIB-SCII *Manual* contains more detailed information on this inventory and its background, and should be studied before the inventory is administered. Considerably more background information on the history and technical issues of interest measurement is reported in the *Handbook for the SVIB* (D. P. Campbell, Stanford University Press, 1971).

Understanding Your Results on the SCII

First, a caution. There is no magic here. Your answers to the test booklet were used to determine your scores: your results are based on what you said you liked or disliked. The results can give you some useful systematic information about yourself, but you should not expect miracles.

More important, *this test does not measure your abilities*; it can tell you something about the patterns in your interests, and how these compare with those of successful people in many occupations, but the results are based on your *interests*, not your abilities. The results may tell you, for example, that you like the way engineers spend their day; they do *not* tell you whether you have a head for the mathematics involved.

Although most of us know something of our own interests, we're not sure how we compare with people actively engaged in various occupations. We don't know "what it would be like" to be a writer, or receptionist, or scientist, or whatever. People using these results are frequently guided to considering occupations they had never given a thought to before. In particular, this inventory may suggest occupations to you that you might find interesting but have never considered before simply because you have not been exposed to them. If you have never heard of cartography, you have probably not thought about a career in mapmaking, even though you might enjoy it. Or the inventory may suggest occupations that you have ignored because you thought they were open only to members of the opposite sex. Sexual barriers are now falling, and virtually all occupations are now open to qualified people of either sex—so don't let imagined barriers rule out your consideration of any occupation.

Men and women, even those in the same occupation, tend to answer some items on the test quite differently. Research has shown that these differences should not be ignored—that separate scales for men and women provide more meaningful results. Generally, the scales for your sex—those marked with the "Sex Norm" corresponding to your sex ("m" or "f")—are more likely to be good predictors for you than scales for the other sex would be. Still, you have been scored on *all* the scales, female and male, so that you can make use of the maximum possible information. In some cases, such as FARMER and SECRETARY, Occupational Scales have not yet been established for both sexes.

How accurate the SCII is in predicting future careers is difficult to say. Studies made of employed people who completed earlier editions of this form as students have shown that about one-half end up in occupations compatible with their profile scores, and most of these like their work. Among those in occupations not compatible with their results, many say they don't like their work, or are doing the job in some unusual manner. In general, profiles with distinct and consistent patterns of high and low scores are better predictors than profiles with scores spread evenly across the middle ranges.

Your answers have been analyzed in three main ways: first, under "General Occupational Themes," for general similarity to six important overall patterns; second, under "Basic Interest Scales," for similarity to clusters of specific activities; third, under "Occupational Scales," for similarity to the interests of men and women in about 100 occupations. The other two groups of data on the profile—in the small blocks labeled "Administrative Indexes" and "Special Scales"—are of interest mainly to your counselor. The first are checks to make certain that you made your marks on the answer sheet clearly and that your answers were processed correctly. The second are scales that have been developed for use in particular settings and require special interpretation; your counselor will discuss them with you.

The Six General Occupational Themes

Psychological research has shown that people can be described in a general way if we relate them to six overall occupational-interest themes. Your scores for these six themes have been calculated from the answers you gave to the questions in the test booklet. The range of these scores is roughly from 30 to 70, with the average person scoring 50. If your score on a given theme is considerably above average, say 60, you share many of the characteristics of that theme; if your score is low, say below 40, you share very few; and if your score is close to the average, you share some characteristics but not many.

Men and women score somewhat differently on some of these themes, and this is taken into account by the printed statement for each score; this statement, which might be, for example,

"This is a MODERATELY HIGH score," is based on a comparison between your scores and the average score for your sex. Thus, you can compare your score either with the scores of a combined male-female sample, by noting your numerical score, or with the scores of only the members of your own sex, by noting the phrasing of the printed comment.

Following are descriptions of the "pure," or extreme, types for the six General Occupational Themes. These descriptions are, most emphatically, only generalizations; none will fit any one person exactly, and in fact most people's interests combine all six themes to some degree or other.

R-THEME: Extreme examples here are rugged, robust, practical, physically strong, and frequently aggressive in outlook; such people usually have good physical skills, but sometimes have trouble expressing themselves in words or in communicating their feelings to others. They like to work outdoors, and they like to work with tools, especially large, powerful machines. They prefer to deal with things rather than with ideas or with people. They generally have conventional political and economic opinions, and are usually cool to radical new ideas. They enjoy creating things with their hands and prefer occupations such as mechanic, construction work, fish and wildlife management, laboratory technician, some engineering specialties, some military jobs, agriculture, or the skilled trades. Although no single word can capture the broad meaning of the entire theme, the word REALISTIC has been used to characterize this pattern, thus the term R-THEME.

I-THEME: This theme tends to center around science and scientific activities. Extremes of this type are task-oriented; they are not particularly interested in working around other people. They enjoy solving abstract problems and have a great need to understand the physical world. They prefer to think through problems rather than act them out. Such people enjoy ambiguous challenges and do not like highly structured situations with many rules. They frequently have unconventional values and attitudes and tend to be original and creative, especially in scientific areas. They prefer occupations such as design engineer, biologist, social scientist, research laboratory worker, physicist, technical writer, or meteorologist. The word INVESTIGATIVE is used to summarize this pattern, thus I-THEME.

A-THEME: The extreme type here is artistically oriented, and likes to work in artistic settings where there are many opportunities for self-expression. Such people have little interest in problems that are highly structured or require gross physical strength, preferring those that can be dealt with through self-expression in artistic media. They resemble I-THEME types in preferring to work alone, but have a greater need for individualistic expression, are usually less assertive about their own opinions and capabilities, and are more sensitive and emotional. They score higher on measures of originality than any of the other types. They describe themselves as independent, original, unconventional, expressive, and tense. Vocational choices include artist, author, cartoonist, composer, singer, dramatic coach, poet, actor or actress, and symphony conductor. This is the ARTISTIC theme, or A-THEME.

S-THEME: The pure types here are sociable, responsible, humanistic, and concerned with the welfare of others. They usually express themselves well and get along well with others; they like attention and seek situations allowing them to be at or near the center of the group. They prefer to solve problems by discussions with others, or by arranging or rearranging relationships between others; they have little interest in situations requiring physical exertion or working with machinery. Such people describe themselves as cheerful, popular, achieving, and good leaders. They prefer occupations such as school superintendent, clinical psychologist, high school teacher, marriage counselor, playground director, speech therapist, or vocational counselor. This is the SOCIAL theme, or S-THEME.

E-THEME: The extreme types here have a great facility with words, which they put to effective use in selling, dominating, and leading; frequently they are in sales work. They see themselves as energetic, enthusiastic, adventurous, self-confident, and dominant, and they prefer social tasks where they can assume leadership. They enjoy persuading others to their viewpoints. They are impatient with precise work or work involving long periods of intellectual effort. They like power, status, and material wealth, and enjoy working in expensive settings. Vocational preferences include business executive, buyer, hotel manager, industrial relations consultant, political campaigner, realtor, many kinds of sales work, sports promoter, and television producer. The word ENTERPRISING summarizes this pattern of interests, thus E-THEME.

C-THEME: Extremes of this type prefer the highly ordered activities, both verbal and numerical, that characterize office work. They fit well into large organizations but do not seek leadership; they respond to power and are comfortable working in a well-established chain of command. They dislike ambiguous situations, preferring to know precisely what is expected of them. Such people describe themselves as conventional, stable, well-controlled, and dependable. They have little interest in problems requiring physical skills or intense relationships with others, and are most effective at well-defined tasks. Like the E-THEME type, they value material possessions and status. Vocational preferences are mostly within the business world, and include bank examiner, bank teller, bookkeeper, some accounting jobs, financial analyst, computer operator, inventory controller, tax expert, statistician, and traffic manager. Although, again, one word cannot adequately represent the entire theme, the word CONVENTIONAL more or less summarizes the pattern, hence C-THEME.

These six themes can be arranged in a hexagon, as shown below, in such a way that themes falling *next* to each other (ENTERPRISING and SOCIAL, for example) are the most similar to each other, whereas those directly *across* the hexagon from each other (REALISTIC and SOCIAL, for example) are the most dissimilar.

REALISTIC   INVESTIGATIVE

CONVENTIONAL ⬡ ARTISTIC

ENTERPRISING   SOCIAL

Few people are "pure" types, scoring high on one theme and low on all the others. Most score high on two, or even three, which means they share some characteristics with each of these; for their career planning, such people should look for an occupational setting that cuts across these patterns.

A few people score low on all six themes; this probably means they have no consistent occupational orientation and would likely be equally comfortable in any of several working environments. But many people, especially young people, score in this manner simply because they haven't had the opportunity to become familiar with a variety of occupational activities.

The Basic Interest Scales

These scales are more or less intermediate between the General Occupational Themes and the Occupational Scales. Each is concerned with one specific area of activity, an area that might partially characterize a General Theme and at the same time be common to a number of occupations. The 23 scales are arranged on the profile in groups corresponding to the strength of their relationships to the six General Themes.

For each scale the level of your score shows how consistently you answered "Like" to the activities in that area. If, for example, you consistently answered "Like" to such items as *Making a speech, Expressing judgments publicly,* and *Be a TV announcer,* then you will have a high score on the PUBLIC SPEAKING scale and you will probably have a higher than average score on the E-THEME. If you consistently answered "Dislike" to these items, you will have a low score on the PUBLIC SPEAKING scale and probably a low score on the E-THEME.

On these scales, the average adult scores about 50, with most people scoring between 30 and 70. If your score for a given scale is substantially higher than that, say about 60, then you have shown more consistent preferences for that kind of activity than the average adult does, and you should look upon that area of activity as an important focus of your interests. The opposite is true for low scores.

As with the other scales, your scores are given both numerically (as a number printed under "Std Score") and graphically (as a mark printed on the grid at the right of the numerical scores). The differences between the sexes in these areas of interest are also displayed graphically: the open bars indicate the middle 50 percent of female scores, the shaded bars the middle 50 percent of male scores. The extending, thinner lines cover the middle 80 percent of scores; and the mark in the middle is the average.

You might find that your scores on some of the Basic Interest Scales appear to be inconsistent with scores on the corresponding Occupational Scales. This can happen—you might, for example, score high on the MATHEMATICS scale and low on the MATHEMATICIAN scale. Scores of this sort are not errors; they are in fact a useful finding. What they usually mean is that although you have a great liking for the subject matter of an occupation (say, mathematics), you share with people in that occupation (mathematicians) very few of their other likes or dislikes, and you would probably not enjoy the day-to-day life of their working world.

The Occupational Scales

Your score on a given Occupational Scale shows how similar your interests are to the interests of people in that occupation. If you reported the same likes and dislikes as they do, your score will be high and you would probably enjoy working in that occupation or a closely related one. If your likes and dislikes are different from those of the people in the occupation, your score will be low and you would not likely be happy in that kind of

work. Remember that the scales for your sex—those marked in the "Sex Norm" column with the sex corresponding to yours—are more likely to be good predictors for you than scales for the other sex would be.

Your score for each scale is printed in numerals and also plotted graphically. Members of an occupation score about 50 on their own scale—that is, female dentists score about 50 on the DENTIST "f" scale, male artists score about 50 on the ARTIST "m" scale, and so forth. If you score high on a particular scale—say 45 or 50—you have many interests in common with the workers in that occupation. The higher your score, the more common interests you have. *But note that on these scales your scores are being compared with those of people working in those occupations;* in the scoring of the General Themes and the Basic Interest Scales you were being compared with "people-in-general." If your score on any of the Occupational Scales is in the "average" range—between 26 and 44—you have responded *in the way people-in-general do.* Scores in this range are therefore of little value in understanding your particular interests, and the profile uses this narrow shaded band to show that such scores should be given little attention.

The Occupational Scales differ from the other scales also in considering your dislikes as well as your likes. If you share the same *dislikes* with the workers in an occupation, you will score moderately high on their scale, even if you don't agree with their *likes.* For example, farmers, artists, and physicists dislike, in general, working with people; if you don't like working with people, you share this with the people in these occupations, and may score fairly high—40, say—on these scales even if you don't like agriculture, art, or science. But a higher score—50, say—reflects an agreement on likes *and* dislikes.

Occupational Groupings

So that the overall pattern of your scores on the Occupational Scales can be better understood, they have been arranged on the profile in six clusters corresponding roughly to the six General Occupational Themes. Within each cluster, occupations expressing more or less similar interests are listed side by side. And because male workers in an occupation sometimes have interests somewhat different from those of female workers in the same occupation, the two scales for that occupation ("m" and "f") may be given on the profile in different groupings.

Just to the left of each Occupational Scale name on the profile are one to three letters indicating the General Themes characteristic of that occupation. These will help you to understand the interest patterns found among the workers in that occupation, and to focus on occupations that might be interesting to you. If you score high on two themes, for example, you should scan the list of Occupational Scales and find any that have the same two theme letters in front of them in any order. If your scores there are also high—as they are likely to be—you should find out more about those occupations, and about related occupations not given on the profile. Your counselor can help you here.

Using Your Scores

Your scores can be used in two main ways: first, to help you understand how your likes and dislikes fit into the world of work; and second, to help you identify possible problems by pointing out areas where your interests differ substantially from those of people working in occupations that you might be considering. Suppose, for example, that you have your heart set on some field of science, and the results show that you have only a moderate interest in the daily exercise of mathematical skills necessary in that setting. Although this is discouraging to learn, you are at least prepared for the choice between (1) abandoning that field of science as a career objective, (2) trying to increase your enthusiasm for mathematics, and (3) finding some branch of the field that requires less use of mathematics.

You have been scored on a broad range of general interests and specific occupations. But you should not become dead set on one particular occupation where your score is high, at least not at an early age; in the world of work there are many hundreds of specialties and professions. Instead, using these results and your scores on other tests as guides, you should search out as much information as you can *about those occupational areas where your interests and aptitudes are focused.* Ask your librarian for information on jobs in these areas, and talk to people working in these fields. Talk with your counselor, who is especially trained to help you, about your results on this test and other tests, and about your future plans. You should recognize that choosing an occupation is not a single decision, but a series of decisions that will go on for many years; whenever a new decision must be made, you should seek the best possible information about yourself and about the work areas you are considering. Your scores on this inventory should help.

students he tested in the 1930s, and from time to time he wrote to them and asked them to take the test again, so that he could find out whether they had changed. Although he did usually find minor changes, and although a few individuals showed completely altered interest pictures at different times, the great majority did not change substantially over periods as long as 22 years. Very recent test-retest reliability data (Campbell, 1977) were collected for three different samples (a two-week sample, a thirty-day sample, and a three-year sample) to determine the stability of the SCII scales. The median test-retest correlations for the two-week, thirty-day, and three-year periods were in the .80's and .90's, indicating that the general occupational themes, the basic interest scales, and the occupational scales are quite stable over short time periods. For longer periods the stability is less, but still very reasonable.

Long-term research has also revealed a great deal about what Strong scores do and do not predict. With a few exceptions such scores do not tell us just how successful a person is likely to be in an occupation or in the training program leading to it. (Perhaps we should never have expected that they would. An individual score expresses how much a person resembles an occupational group made up entirely of those successful enough to stay in the field. Degrees of success are not considered.) What the scores do predict is how likely individuals are to remain in particular occupations or shift to others. Further, although some studies indicate that the correlation between interest scores and self-rated job satisfaction is not very high, evidence suggests that those who are in occupations on which they obtained high Strong scores are on the whole better satisfied with their positions than are others whose interest scores did not point in the particular direction they took.

As previously mentioned, Holland's Vocational Preference Inventory initially defined his theoretical personality types and model environments, and led to the development of the very practical and useful Self Directed Search (SDS). The SDS was developed to fill the need in the field of counseling for a reasonably short, self-administered, self-scored and self-interpreted inventory which would reflect a person's interests and relate them to appropriate occupational groups. The SDS was then a vocational-counseling experience for people who did not have access to professional counselors or could not afford their services. In its present form the SDS is composed of two parts. The first part is an assessment booklet (228 items) which asks the individual to report occupational daydreams, preferences for various activities and occupations, competencies in performing various tasks, and self-estimates of abilities. From these self-reported activities, competencies, occupations and self-ratings one obtains a summary code representing an individual's resemblance to each of the six personality types. In the second part of the inventory, the individual is directed to use the occupational classification booklet containing 456 occupational titles (95 percent of the labor market in the United States) to identify occupational groups corresponding to the summary code (highest three scores). The user is encouraged to use all combinations of the three-letter code (ISE) in the search for occupations.

The various assessment methods of the SDS are included for different reasons. The occupational-daydreams section encourages the individual to engage in some occupational exploration, and may be used to predict a person's future occupation. The six activity scales are measures—of personal involvement and how people spend their time—that are characteristic of each type. The six competency scales are self-reported estimates of a person's proficiencies and aptitudes. The six occupation scales are measures of occupational preferences. Finally, the two sets of self-estimates consist of self-ratings (talents and traits) found to be most identified with one type.

One very positive feature of the SDS is the recent research exploring the impact and the effects of the SDS on students and clients. This is one of the few inventories that has been studied to determine the effects of its use with people. These investigations have shown that the SDS has positive influences on both men and women and that these positive effects are similar to those of counselors. The positive effects on people take the form of expanding vocational alternatives, reinforcing a current vocational alternative, stimulating vocational exploration, reducing indecision, and stimulating more satisfaction with choice. The above effects clearly indicate that the SDS has positive beneficial influences for users.

Many validity studies, primarily concurrent in nature, have been carried out on Holland's SDS. In the main this evidence shows that college students tend to enter college-major environments consistent with their dominant personality types. Other work, again using college students, suggests that students in college-major environments consistent with their personality types tend to report being more stable (personally and vocationally) and satisfied. Students reporting educational programs inconsistent with their personality types do not seem to be as well off in terms of their academic and personal adjustment. Some work has explored the interests of working populations using the SDS. The evidence here suggests that the SDS may be successfully applied in work environments. In other words, men and women tend to work in occupational environments consistent with their personality types, and these findings tend to obtain for white and black men and women.

Another inventory used in the counseling of persons is the Kuder Occupational Interest Survey (KOIS) (Kuder, 1968). The KOIS is a well-constructed interest inventory that has lacked extensive investigation of its predictive validity—a limitation that is currently being corrected. A unique feature of the KOIS is the college-major scales; no other interest inventory has such scales. In its present form, the KOIS is a 100 triad inventory asking the respondent to choose in each triad the one activity preferred most and the activity preferred least. The individual's preferences are then compared with the responses of many occupational and college-major groups. The thought is that an individual who has an interest pattern similar to the interest pattern of people in a particular occupation is likely to find satisfaction in that occupation. On the report form (see Figure 20) the numbers to the right of the titles indicate the individual's scores. Testees are scored on all scales regardless of the sex-grouped norms, and the main headings at the top of the report form indicate whether the scale was developed from the responses of males or of females. The individual's highest scores are reported at the bottom of the report form (see Figure 21) in order to aid the interpretation of the results. All scores above the line of dashes in each column of ranked scores are within .06 of the individual's highest score in that column and may be considered nearly equivalent. These are the individual's highest scores and should be given primary consideration. The greater the difference between two scores, the greater the difference in the testee's preferences and those of people actually in occupations or college majors. About 80 percent of people actually in the occupations or college majors listed score .45 or higher on the scale for their job or field of study. In general, the interpretive leaflet suggests that most students have some scores over .40. The manual contains additional information on background, development and interpretation.

A recent follow-up study by Zytowski (1976) revealed considerable information about what the KOIS scores do predict. He contacted 882 men and women 12 to 19 years after they had taken an early form of the Kuder Occupational Interest Survey either in high school or college. The follow-up data show that 50 percent of the total group were employed in an occupation that would have been suggested to them had the inventory been interpreted 12 to 19 years previously. In looking at the predictive validity of the college-major scales, Zytowski found it to be slightly superior to that of the occupational scales. The college-major scales from a high school administration correctly predicted the third-year college major of 55 percent of the students. The average span of prediction represented

Report of Scores — *Kuder Occupational Interest Survey* (Form DD)

NAME ______________________ LOCATION ______________________ DATE OF SURVEY ____________

OCCUPATIONAL SCALES FEMALE NORMS		COLLEGE MAJOR SCALES, FEMALE	OCCUPATIONAL SCALES MALE NORMS				COLLEGE MAJOR SCALES MALE NORMS	
					Optometrist .24	Psychology Professor .31		
Accountant .30	Nurse .29	Art & Art Education .42	Acc't, Certified Public .17	Engineer, Electrical .25	Osteopath .24	Radio Station Manager .20	Agriculture .25	Foreign Languages .42
Bank Clerk .24	Nutritionist .38	Biological Sciences .43	Architect .39	Engineer, Heating Air Cond. .25	Painter, House .22	Real Estate Agent .19	Animal Husbandry .28	Forestry .30
Beautician .26	Occupational Therapist .39	Business Ed & Commerce .27	Automobile Mechanic .19	Engineer, Industrial .18	Pediatrician .33	Sales Eng, Heating/Air Cond. .18	Architecture .39	History .29
Bookkeeper .24	Office Clerk .24	Drama .36	Automobile Salesperson .11	Engineer, Mechanical .24	Personnel Manager .19	Science Teacher, High School .29	Art & Art Education .41	Law (Grad School) .24
Bookstore Manager .41	Physical Therapist .41	Elementary Education .35	Banker .19	Engineer, Mining & Metal .29	Pharmaceutical Salesperson .13	School Superintendent .25	Biological Sciences .33	Mathematics .29
Computer Programmer .44	Primary School Teacher .34	English .38	Bookkeeper .18	Farmer .23	Pharmacist .22	Social Caseworker .29	Business Acc't & Finance .14	Music & Music Ed .48
Counselor, High School .31	Psychologist .39	Foreign Languages .44	Bookstore Manager .32	Florist .25	Photographer .26	Social Worker, Group .29	Business & Marketing .14	Physical Education .22
Dean of Women .38	Psychologist, Clinical .39	General Social Sciences .34	Bricklayer .20	Forester .27	Physical Therapist .26	Social Worker, Psychiatric .29	Business Management .15	Physical Sciences .33
Dental Assistant .26	Religious Education Director .36	Health Professions .38	Building Contractor .23	Insurance Agent .15	Physician .25	Statistician .31	Economics .18	Political Science & Gov't .24
Department Store Salesperson .22	Science Teacher, High School .37	History .42	Buyer .18	Interior Decorator .37	Plumber .18	Supervisor, Industrial .22	Elementary Education .32	Premed, Pharm & Dentistry .24
Dietitian, Administrative .33	Secretary .28	Home Economics Education .38	Carpenter .18	Journalist .25	Plumbing Contractor .17	Travel Agent .23	Engineering, Chemical .23	Psychology .25
Dietitian, Public School .33	Social Caseworker .40	Mathematics .41	Chemist .32	Lawyer .28	Podiatrist .20	Truck Driver .12	Engineering, Civil .25	Sociology .28
Florist .32	Social Worker, Group .39	Music & Music Education .49	Clothier, Retail .17	Librarian .38	Policeman .15	Television Repairer .22	Engineering, Electrical .26	U.S. Air Force Cadet .22
Home Demonstration Agent .34	Social Worker, Medical .36	Nursing .33	Computer Programmer .32	Machinist .19	Police Officer .19	University Pastor .30	Engineering, Mechanical .23	U.S. Military Cadet .20
Home Ec Teacher, College .37	Social Worker, Pyschiatric .39	Physical Education .38	Counselor, High School .25	Mathematician .37	Printer .21	Veterinarian .26	English .35	
Interior Decorator .39	Social Worker, School .38	Political Science .35	County Agricultural Agent .26	Math Teacher, High School .28	Psychiatrist .30	Welder .21		
Lawyer .32	Stenographer .26	Psychology .40	Dentist .26	Meteorologist .33	Psychologist, Clinical .29	X-Ray Technician .26		
Librarian .39	X-Ray Technician .31	Sociology .32	Electrician .19	Minister .32	Psychologist, Counseling .24	YMCA Secretary .21		
Math Teacher, High School .34		Teaching Sister, Catholic .26	Engineer, Civil .27	Nursery Worker, Plant .31	Psychologist, Industrial .20			

OCCUPATIONAL SCALES FEMALE NORMS		COLLEGE MAJOR SCALES FEMALE NORMS		OCCUPATIONAL SCALES MALE NORMS		COLLEGE MAJOR SCALES MALE NORMS	
Title	Score	Title	Score	Title	Score	Title	Score

V ________

M ______	S ______
MBI ______	F ______
W ______	D ______
WBI	MO

Figure 20. Report of scores for the Kuder Occupational Interest Survey, Form DD for Eliza Johnson. *Source: Kuder DD Occupational Interest Survey Interpretive Leaflet. Chicago, Illinois: Science Research Associates, 1974. Copyright 1974 by Science Research Associates, and reproduced with permission.*

OCCUPATIONAL SCALES FEMALE NORMS		COLLEGE MAJOR SCALES FEMALE NORMS		OCCUPATIONAL SCALES MALE NORMS		COLLEGE MAJOR SCALES MALE NORMS	
Title	Score	Title	Score	Title	Score	Title	Score
COMPUTR PROGRAMR	.41	MATHEMATICS	.43	BRICKLAYER	45	FORESTRY	.51
PHYS THERAPIST	.39	PHYSICAL EDUC	.43	FORESTER	44	ENGINEERING, MECH	.49
X-RAY TECHNICIAN	.38	HEALTH PROFES	.40	AUTO MECHANIC	43	ENGINEERING, CIVIL	.48
OCCUPA THERAPIST	.36	BIOLOGICAL SCI	.39	PAINTER, HOUSE	43	ENGINEERING, ELEC	.48
				PHOTOGRAPHER	43	ANIMAL HUSBANDRY	.46
FLORIST	.34	MUSIC & MUSIC ED	.36	POSTAL CLERK	43	AGRICULTURE	.45
BANK CLERK	.33			X-RAY TECHNICIAN	43		
BOOKKEEPER	.33			COMPUTR PROGRAMR	42	ARCHITECTURE	.44
STENOGRAPHER	.33			ELECTRICIAN	42	MATHEMATICS	.43
BEAUTICIAN	.32			ENGINEER, CIVIL	42	PHYSICAL SCIENCE	.43
DENTAL ASSISTANT	.32					MUSIC & MUSIC ED	.41

Figure 21. Scores from the Kuder Occupational Interest Survey, Form DD for Alan Kahn. *Source: Kuder Occupational Interest Survey Interpretive Leaflet. Chicago, Illinois: Science Research Associates, 1974. Copyright 1974 by Science Research Associates, and reproduced with permission.*

five years, with a range from three to eight. Or stated another way, more than half of the students who had decided on a major in college were correctly predicted by a scale in the top .06 range on the KOIS administered during high school. If the top .12 range of scores on the KOIS is used, four-fifths of the students are correctly predicted. However, in another vein the scores do not say much about self-reported satisfaction or success. Individuals in occupations consistent with their early interest profiles did not report greater job satisfaction or success, but did demonstrate more persistence in their occupational careers. Other evidence suggests that better prediction is achieved when the individual has attended or graduated from college or entered a high-level occupation.

Some earlier work by Kuder and Zytowski demonstrates reasonable concurrent validity for the KOIS. Kuder found that 34 percent of a group of men in varied occupations scored highest on their own KOIS occupational scale. Zytowski's results were very similar, finding that 35 percent of a varied group scored highest on their own scale. More recently Zytowski (1977) explored the effects of receiving the results of the KOIS on several aspects of vocational behavior among 157 eleventh and twelfth grade high school students. He found that receiving results increased self-knowledge, when compared to a control group that received no results. However, KOIS results did not affect confidence in or satisfaction with vocational plans, unless the person had reported high interest in the inventory results beforehand. In sum, the above information on the KOIS clearly indicates that the inventory may be used with more confidence than previously believed. The predictive work and effects work by Zytowski was a major advancement in the practical use of this inventory.

A few more words about the previously mentioned MMPI, Minnesota Multiphasic Personality Inventory (1967), seem appropriate as

94

we talk about widely used inventories. There is little question that the MMPI is the most useful single psychological test available in clinical and counseling settings for assessing the degree and nature of emotional upset. As the manual indicates, it was designed to assess some major personality characteristics that affect personal and social adjustment. It is a long inventory containing some 550 statements covering a range of subject matter such as physical condition, moral attitude, and social attitudes. Originally, the inventory was composed of nine scales named for the psychiatric-psychological condition assessed: Hs (Hypochondriasis), D (Depression), Hy (Hysteria), Pd (Psychopathic Deviate), Mf (Masculinity-Femininity), Pa (Paranoia), Pt (Psychoasthenia), Sc (Schizophrenia), and Ma (Hypomania). A variety of other scales—for example, Si (Social Introversion), Es (Ego Strength), Dy (Dependency), Lb (Low Back Pain), A (Anxiety Factor)— have been developed over the years, and these added scales have made the inventory useful for assessing other variables (for example, degree of anxiety, ego strength) that tend to be independent of the diagnostic classification. There are three validity scales or scales concerned with faking: L (Lie), F (Validity) and K (Correction). These scales attempt to pick up distorted responses, a fake-sick response set, and a defensiveness response style. A high score on a scale is defined as one that is two standard deviations (above T score of 70) above the normal population mean (See Figure 22).

The MMPI scales were developed by contrasting the responses of normal groups with the responses of clinical cases. As far as validity is concerned, the findings show that a high scale score has been found to positively predict the associated clinical diagnosis in more than 60 percent of new psychiatric admissions. In general, a high scale score on the MMPI is suggestive of the presence of the trait and the related symptoms. Machine scoring and computer interpretation are popular with the MMPI. A computer printout of profile and interpretation is shown in Figure 22.

Another personality inventory that has been widely used in a variety of research and practical situations (bibliographies assembled by the author, Harrison G. Gough, report a total of more than 600 publications by early 1969) is the California Psychological Inventory (CPI). In order to come out with a test that would be useful in many situations—schools as well as clinics, correctional institutions as well as mental hospitals, for example—Gough started out with items representing what he calls "folk concepts," the ideas about personality that people are accustomed to use as they size one another up and attempt to forecast what other people are likely to do, rather

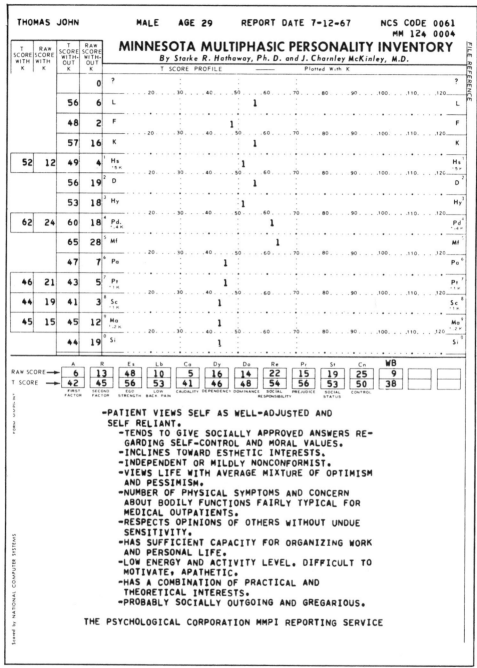

Figure 22. Computer printout of profile and interpretation for the MMPI. *Source: S. R. Hathaway and J. C. McKinley. Minnesota Multiphasic Personality Inventory Manual Revised 1967. New York, New York: The Psychological Corporation, 1970. Copyright 1970 by The Psychological Corporation, and reproduced with permission.*

than with concepts based on an esoteric personality theory or on psychiatric classifications. Using item analysis techniques for comparing special kinds of people with ordinary people—juvenile delinquents, for example, with nondelinquent boys and girls of the same age—Gough produced an inventory that can be scored for eighteen different traits:

  ✓ I.   Measures of Poise, Ascendancy, Self-Assurance, and Interpersonal Adequacy
      1. *Do* Dominance
      2. *Cs* Capacity for status
      3. *Sy* Sociability
      4. *Sp* Social Presence
      5. *Sa* Self-acceptance
      6. *Wb* Sense of well-being

  II.   Measures of Socialization, Maturity, Responsibility, and Intrapersonal Structuring of Values
      7. *Re* Responsibility
      8. *So* Socialization
      9. *Sc* Self-control
    10. *To* Tolerance
    11. *Gi* Good impression
    12. *Cm* Communality

  III. Measures of Achievement Potential and Intellectual Efficiency
    13. *AC* Achievement via conformance
    14. *Ai* Achievement via independence
    15. *Ie* Intellectual efficiency

  IV. Measures of Intellectual and Interest Modes
    16. *Py* Psychological-mindedness
    17. *Fx* Flexibility
    18. *Fe* Femininity

Figure 23 shows what an individual's profile of scores looks like.

    The extensive bibliography referred to above provides evidence that the CPI can indeed be used for the practical purposes the author designed it to serve—to predict, for example, which bright students are not likely to consider going to college unless special efforts are made to bring this possibility to their attention, or which of the young people from a poverty area are most likely to become delinquents if they are not given special help or attention. One interesting sidelight on this test is that it has been translated into a number of European and Asiatic languages, and at least some of the scales have been found to be as predictive of actual behavior in Italy, Japan, or India as they are in the United States.

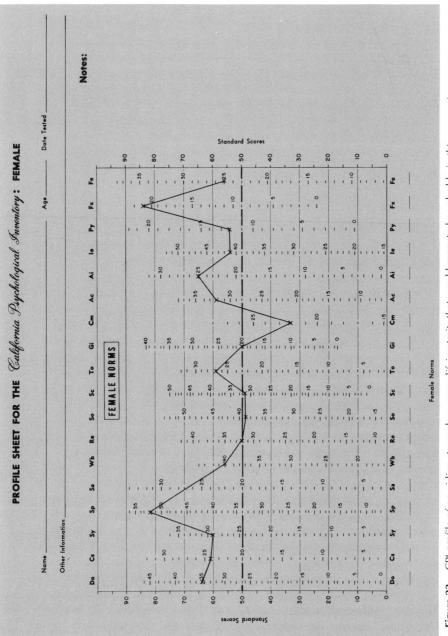

Figure 23. CPI profile of an airline stewardess exemplifying traits that would seem to be valuable in this occupation—poise, tolerance, independence, and flexibility. *(Reproduced with permission from the Manual for The California Psychological Inventory by Harrison G. Gough, p. 15. Copyright 1959 by Consulting Psychologists Press, Inc., Palo Alto, Calif.)*

PROJECTIVE TECHNIQUES

Let us turn now to the other main branch of personality testing, the projective methods. With these, instead of asking the testee questions, the examiner presents some ambiguous stimulus and asks the testee to interpret it or react to it. Inkblots and pictures of human situations have been used most commonly. (See Figure 24.) Since an inkblot is not really a picture of anything, the interpretation a person gives must come from the way the individual perceives and organizes the world. Similarly, since the picture in Figure 24 does not make it clear what the two persons are doing or saying to one another, any story one makes up about it must stem from one's thoughts and feelings. This suggests the reason for the label of this type of test: One is said to *project* into the picture one's own emotional attitudes and ideas about life. Some have argued that *self-expressive* would be a better overall designation for these methods, but the title *projective* is old and it has stuck.

The first of these tests to be widely used, and still probably the most popular of them all, is the Rorschach test. This is a set of ten inkblots of various shapes. Some are black and white only; some have color as well. The subject is asked to tell what he or she sees in each one. After the subject has responded, the examiner asks as many questions as are needed to make clear just what the subject saw in the blot and what aspect of it determined the individual's perceptions. Since 1921 when Hermann Rorschach, a Swiss psychiatrist, proposed this technique, a number of somewhat different scoring systems have been developed, and a tremendous number of books and journal articles have been written about it. The various scoring systems provide for separate analysis of the structure, or style, of the responses and of their content. *Structure* has to do with such questions as: How productive is the person in responding to this sort of stimulus? In other words, does the subject have many responses or few to each card? Does the subject usually react to each figure as a whole or to its parts? To what extent does the subject base responses on form, color, and shading? *Content* pertains to the extent to which the person sees the blots as human figures, animals, anatomical diagrams, maps, clouds, or other concrete things. The degree to which a person tends to give either popular or original responses is also of some interest.

It should be evident from even this brief description of the many aspects to analyze in an individual's responses to inkblots that the job of interpretation is a highly complex undertaking. For one thing, there is no way in which a test like this can be validated all at once. As research studies have accumulated over the years, it has become apparent that a good many of the inferences clinicians were once accustomed to make on the basis of this test were unjustified. It has not proved to be the "Open Sesame" to personality secrets that its more enthusiastic practitioners thought it was going to be. But in spite of inadequacies, it is still a valuable tool for practicing clinicians. Used along with other techniques for assessing personality, such as interviews and background information, it furnishes clues about matters that can profitably be explored in studying an individual case. The Holtzman Ink Blots, brought out in 1961, correct some of the deficiencies of the Rorschach technique while keeping many of its advantages.

Another widely used projective technique is the Thematic Apperception Test (TAT). This consists of cards showing pictures of people. The situation in each case and how the persons are feeling about it are purposely left undefined so that the testees can "read in" their own attitudes and ways of perceiving the world. The testee's task is to make up a story for each picture, including in the account some explanation of what led to the illustrated situation, what the characters are thinking and feeling, and what the outcome will be. Figure 24 shows a picture similar to those used in the TAT.

As with the Rorschach, many ways of analyzing and interpreting a person's TAT stories have been explored. Generally, though, the examiner looks first to see which character has been made the protagonist of the story, since that is probably the person with whom the storyteller identifies. The examiner then studies the details of each story carefully—what the subject said and how—deriving hypotheses therefrom about the individual's needs, feelings, and attitudes, and noting how often the same trends occur in different stories. Most clinicians use this information as a basis for a verbal description of the testee rather than a score or set of scores. Researchers, however, give overall ratings for the personality traits in which they are interested.

The research possibilities in this general method have been exploited in many ways. Special sets of pictures for children and persons from other cultures have been tried. Methods of scoring for specific characteristics have been standardized. A good example of the use of the storytelling method in research is the work of McClelland and his associates on *achievement* motivation, to which we referred earlier. They presented to their research subjects pictures carefully selected to stimulate the invention of stories about achievement. Then they analyzed each person's stories according to a standardized system. They considered the desires the main character expresses, the activity engaged in, and the obstacles encountered,

Figure 24. A picture similar to those used in projective personality tests. *(Photo courtesy of Standard Oil Company of New Jersey.)*

along with several other features. Thus, they obtained a score for each subject on Achievement Need. In a continuing program of research they have been studying the ways in which these scores relate to the people's backgrounds and subsequent achievements.

We could mention many other particular varieties of projective tests, but any complete discussion would carry us far beyond our present interests. One thing we can say of all the projective tests: Their validation is incomplete. They are not therefore ready to be automatically applied in making decisions about people in practical situations as teachers, social workers, and employment managers must do. In the hands of a competent psychologist with a wide background of knowledge about personality structure and functioning, they can often contribute to such decisions. But there is no way in which a person can attain skill in the use of projective tests without this background. Taking a single course in Projective Techniques certainly does not provide it.

Perhaps the greatest value of projective techniques lies in the contribution they make to research on personality, for they allow psychologists to get some clues about things people are not able to talk about directly—their underlying motives, assumptions, and ways of looking at the world.

FROM MEASUREMENT TO ASSESSMENT

One hears less and less about personality *measurement* these days and more about personality *assessment*. To what kind of change in our thinking does this shift in terminology correspond? It is, first of all, a recognition that personality is inherently complex and many-faceted. It does not seem likely that we will ever be able to character-ize personality by a score or any combination of scores. The term *assessment* suggests a broader, more comprehensive survey of an individual than *measurement* does.

In addition to standardized tests, the most common and time-honored methods for making such assessments are observations, in-terviews, and ratings. Their main weaknesses arise mainly from the fact that the personality of the *observer* as well as that of the *ob-served* shows up in the evaluation. However, knowing that any single description of a person may be biased or inaccurate, one can still use combinations of these techniques to obtain material for sound personality assessments.

Assessment research has led to techniques in which observa-tional and psychometric approaches are combined. Items of bio-graphical material included on application blanks, for example, can be *scored* by making use of group comparisons like those used for developing empirical scoring keys on personality inventories. By comparing highly successful insurance salesmen, for example, with men who do not do well, it is possible to identify a set of entries on application blanks that have predictive value for this occupation. Another way of combining old and new approaches is to have one's subjects rated by others, but standardize the *situation* in which they are to be observed. If they are brought together in a discussion group or given some challenging task to carry out, observations made in these situations may be more accurate than those made under the varying circumstances of everyday life.

A number of other approaches to personality assessment have been explored, but the examples given above are sufficient to illus-trate the point that there are other ways besides tests to size up what individuals are like—how each typically thinks, feels, and reacts to the circumstances of life. It is not important that we be able to measure personality; it is important that we be able to assess it.

SOME GENERAL CONSIDERATIONS

As more and more research results have been reported, psychologists have been forced to recognize that behavior we consider to be a manifestation of personality traits is not highly predictable. The reason seems to be that as we grow up, we acquire a repertory of roles we can play, an assortment of somewhat different "personalities." Frequently the way we behave is more closely related to the situational context than it is to our inner needs and motives. We recognize that Mr. Jenkins reveals one sort of "personality" in talking to his wife and quite a different one in talking to his boss. We realize that the most thorough personality assessment we can make will not enable us to predict with even reasonable accuracy how well a mental hospital patient is likely to get along when discharged from the hospital, unless we know a good deal about the situation at home. Personality assessment techniques contribute to our understanding of people—ourselves and others. They should not be expected to do more than this.

Vocational Psychology and Assessment

7

Theories of vocational behavior have developed over the years in an attempt to understand the process of vocational development and how people learn different vocational behaviors and make data-based career decisions. In general, the theories that have emerged help people organize and understand information (personality, interests, abilities, etc.) about themselves and their social environments. The theories help people assess self and environment in order that they may cope more effectively and interact in social environments consistent with personality style.

In their attempts to assess and understand vocational behavior and the vocational choice process, the various theories have assumed different perspectives. Some theories have viewed vocational behavior from an interactional perspective. These theories (Holland, 1973; Stern, 1970) assume that vocational development is a function of the person and the social environment, and specification of vocational development from this perspective attempts to consider aspects of both. Unfortunately, person-environment interaction is most difficult to assess. Nevertheless, these theories suggest that assessment of the person is incomplete without some assessment of the environment. Again unfortunately, these theories have little to say about the physical features of the environment, natural and constructed; their emphasis is primarily on the social environment as it is perceived and reported by the people interacting in it.

A second perspective assumed by a number of theories is the

more traditional person perspective (Super, 1953; Roe, 1957; Osipow, 1973). These theories focus on the individual's personal characteristics (personality) outside of the immediate interaction. The thought is that personality characteristics will link the individual to different vocational environments. Each individual is believed to have a characteristic level of different personality dimensions that are fairly constant (or at least the rank order is stable) from one context to another. On the stability issue, there is evidence that has accumulated over the years suggesting that some human characteristics may be more stable than others. On a continuum of high stability to low stability, physical variables (height, weight, sight, and hearing) are probably the most stable in different situations; ability variables (intelligence, verbal, math, and dexterity) probably rank second; intersts (social, science, conventional, artistic, and enterprising) third; and personality variables (dominance, honesty, sociability, and flexibility) fourth. It seems that at least some personality variables are more affected by situational differences than others. In any event, the person perspective has accounted for the development of many assessment devices permitting some linkage from the individual to various vocational environments.

A third perspective is the situational or environmental perspective. The theories associated with this perspective (Barker, 1968; Moos, 1976) suggest that vocational behavior is a function of environmental or situational variables. The environment or the context is the determining variable, and the individual's behavior tends to vary from one context or social environment to another. This perspective holds that vocational behavior is environmentally specific and, in general, that different environmental situations will tend to stimulate different behavior.

There are other perspectives and different ways of viewing the theories of career development, but the above scheme seems most meaningful. This chapter, then, focuses on the field of vocational psychology as it reflects the convergence of theory, assessment, and research. Thus, selected theories of vocational psychology are considered that have implications for assessment and application.

THE INTERACTIONAL PERSPECTIVE

The interactional perspective may be viewed as a synthesis of person and environment in which the interaction of the two is the main source of vocational behavior. This position may be expressed as VB = f(P,E), where *VB* stands for Vocational Behavior, *P* for Person, and

E for Environment. Some theories mirroring this perspective are Holland's *Personality Types and Model Environments* and Stern's *Need × Press = Culture* theory.

Holland's Theory of Personality Types and Model Environment

Holland's (1973) theory is based on the notion that vocational behavior is a function of personality and social environment. The theory emphasizes interests and personality, since to Holland the choice of an occupation is an expression of personality, thus making interest inventories personality inventories. The environmental component of the theory is pinned to the notion that people in a particular vocational environment tend to have similar personalities and histories of personal development. Because people in a given vocational environment have like personalities, it is thought that they tend to cope in similar ways.

More specifically, Holland attempts to explain vocational behavior by using a few well-defined ideas. First, people learn to be one or more personality types. A type is defined as a cluster of personal attributes which may be used to assess the person. His six types are described below.

The Realistic(R) type likes realistic jobs such as that of the automobile mechanic, farmer, or electrician. They have mechanical abilities and tend to be conforming, honest, materialistic, natural, persistent, practical, modest, and stable.

The Investigative(I) type likes investigative jobs such as that of the chemist, physicist, biologist, or geologist. I's have mathematical and scientific ability and are described as analytical, independent, intellectual, introverted, methodical, and rational.

The Artistic(A) type likes artistic jobs such as that of the musician, writer, or actor. A's have writing, music, and/or artistic abilities and are described as complicated, emotional, expressive, imaginative, impulsive, nonconforming, and original.

The Social(S) type likes social jobs such as that of the teacher, counseling psychologist, clinical psychologist, or speech therapist. S's have social skills and are described as cooperative, friendly, helpful, insightful, responsible, sociable, and understanding.

The Enterprising(E) type likes enterprising jobs such as that of the salesperson, manager, or business executive. E's have leadership and verbal abilities and are described as ambitious, domineering, pleasure seeking, self-confident, and sociable.

The Conventional(C) type likes conventional jobs such as that of the bookkeeper, banker, or tax expert. C's have clerical and arithmetic ability and are described as conforming, conscientious, orderly, persistent, practical, and self-controlled.

A person's resemblance to each of the personality types is assessed by the use of the Vocational Preference Inventory (VPI), the Self Directed Search (SDS), and the Strong-Campbell Interest Inventory (SCII), which were discussed in Chapter Six.

A second idea used by Holland to explain vocational behavior is that vocational environments in which people live and work may be characterized by their resemblance to one or more model environments. Six model vocational environments are suggested, corresponding to the personality types. For each personality type there is a related environment. The idea is that Artistic types tend to search for and enter Artistic environments and that Investigative types move toward and enter Investigative environments, and so on. Vocational environments are assessed for their resemblance to each of six environmental models by use of the Environmental Assessment Technique. This measurement technique entails taking a census of self-reported vocational preference, college major choice, or current work activity of the members of a population. Each vocational preference, college-major choice, or work activity may then be coded and the dominant model environment identified.

A third idea used by Holland is that congruent person-environment interactions (an Artistic personality type in an Artistic environment) lead to outcomes that are predictable and understandable from the knowledge of personality types and model environments. These outcomes include vocational choice, vocational stability, personal stability, and satisfaction.

Holland further suggests that the relations among types, among environments, and between types and environments tend to be hexagonal in nature. (See Figure 25.) Types and environments that are in closest proximity in the hexagon figure are more psychologically related. Types and environments that are further removed from one another are more psychologically different. For example, an Artistic person in an Artistic vocational environment is in a more congruent situation than an Artistic person in a Social vocational environment. An Artistic person in a Conventional vocational environment is in the most incongruent situation possible.

In general, the research based on Holland's ideas supports the existence of the personality types and model vocational environments. Evidence indicates that individuals tend to choose, enter, and persist in college-major environments and occupational environments consistent with their personality types. For example, Enterprising people tend to choose, enter, and remain in Enterprising occupational environments. Other evidence indicates that congruent person-environment interactions are conducive to personal and vocational stability and satisfaction.

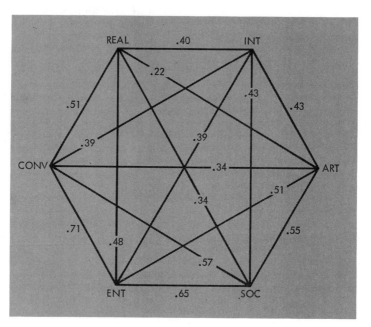

Figure 25. A hexagonal model for interpreting inter and intra-class relationships. *Source: J. L. Holland. Professional Manual for the Self Directed Search. Palo Alto, California: Consulting Psychologists Press, 1972. Copyright 1972 by the Consulting Psychologists Press, and reproduced with permission.*

Additional meaningful data about adolescents and adults implies that person-environment congruence and job satisfaction increase with age. Thus, it seems that people in congruent work situations will probably change little, because their expression of interests, abilities, and personality is rewarded. Persons in incongruent work environments will probably change the most, since they tend to be ignored and punished (Holland, 1976). This work, then, indicates that students and workers that tend to be functioning in environments consistent with their personal characteristics probably are psychologically healthier and more satisfied when compared to people in incongruent situations.

Stern's *Need* × *Press* = *Culture* Theory

Stern's theory, although outside of the main theoretical stream of vocational psychology, does have some meaningful implications for assessing people in work situations. The foundation of Stern's theoretical approach is based upon the work of Lewin (1936), who contended that scientific psychology must take into account the whole situation, defined as the state of both person and environment. Within the Lewinian frame of reference, Murray (1938) developed a need-press model based on the assumption that behavior is an outcome of the relationship between the person (needs) and the environment (presses). Stern (1970), in his work, operationally defined the important concepts of Murray's need-press model.

Three ideas underlie Stern's assessment of people in context. The first and basic idea drawn from Lewin is that behavior is a function of the relationship between the individual and the environment. The second notion is that the psychological significance of the person may be inferred from behavior. In Murray's need-press model, the person is represented in terms of needs, as indicated by self-reported behavior. A need state is characterized by the tendency to perform actions of a certain kind. Thirty needs (Achievement, Adaptability, Dominance, Nurturance, Objectivity, Order, etc.) are described and assessed by Stern (1970) using the Activities Index. The third idea is that the psychological significance of the environment may be inferred from behavioral perceptions. In the need-press model, the environment is defined in terms of presses inferred from self-reported perceptions of the environment. Stern defined press as the characteristic demands or features of the environment as perceived by those who live in the particular environment. Thus, the environment is defined as it is collectively perceived and reported by its participants. To assess environment, four indexes were developed—College Characteristics Index, High School Characteristics Index, Evening College Characteristics Index, and the Organizational Climate Index. The press concept provides an external parallel to the internalized personality needs; for each personality need there is a related press.

Much of the research in the need-press framework has simply attempted to identify need commonalities and/or differences between various vocational groups. For example, some research (Stern, 1970) assessing medical students found that students oriented toward service were more outgoing than research-oriented students, but less aggressive and nonconforming than students who were psychiatrically oriented. Students oriented toward surgery seemed to be more conforming, achievement oriented, and orderly than those choosing psychiatry. Other studies have found differences in personality patterns of teachers, counselors, academic-major groups, athletes, and students in different types of colleges when compared to college students in general.

Some additional work of interest has linked Stern's ideas to Holland's personality types and model environments. Bohn (1966) related needs inferred from responses on an adjective checklist to

Holland's personality types. Conventional people, for example, were found to be high on achievement, order, affiliation, dominance, endurance, and defensiveness needs; Enterprising people were high on achievement, exhibition, affiliation, dominance, and heterosexual needs. Astin and Holland (1961) related the Environmental Assessment Technique (EAT) measure with the College Characteristic Index (CCI) press scales across 36 colleges and found significant correlations between matching scales. For example, the EAT Artistic measure correlated .69 with the CCI Sensuality scale, and the Enterprising measure correlated .79 with the Humanities, Social Science scale. Or, stated another way, colleges with large percentages of Investigative students tended to be rated low on Deference but high on Fantasied Achievement, Objectivity, and Understanding. Thus, Investigative environments seemed to reward independence of thought and action, the need to achieve, and the need to analyze and understand.

The most recent research, and perhaps the most relevant, suggests some congruence between student needs and environmental presses. Using the AI and the CCI to assess needs and presses, Cohn (1966) conducted a factor analysis across 55 colleges and unversities, which produced five college cultures (similar, at least in name, to Holland's personality types and environments): Expressive (Artistic), Intellectual (Investigative), Protective (Conventional), Vocational (Realistic), and Collegiate (Social/Enterprising). A college culture is defined as a composite of the environmental press and the needs of its inhabitants. These findings indicate that students characterized by a certain need pattern tend to be found at institutions with appropriate press. Thus, the results indicate that behavior to some extent may be functionally related to needs and perceived environmental pressures. Stern further suggests that, in his opinion, in some settings press variables may be stronger than need variables, but in other settings need variables may be stronger than press variables. Stated more simply, in some settings the environment tends to shape behavior, but in other settings the individual is the prime determinant of behavior.

A next logical step is to extend the findings to work environments. In any event, the evidence to some extent implies that workers characterized by a certain need pattern may be found in work environments with appropriate work pressures.

THE PERSON PERSPECTIVE

Theories couched in the person perspective focus upon the individual as the crucial variable in the vocational development process. The individual's traits, psychic structures, self-concept, or inner disposition are viewed as the main determinants of behavior and, in general, the environment is viewed as additive rather than interactive. This perspective may be expressed as $VB = f(P)$, where VB stands for Vocational Behavior and P for Person. Adhering to this person emphasis and discussed here are the Trait-Factor, Self-Concept, and Personality approaches.

Trait-Factor Approach

The Trait-Factor approach (Osipow, 1973), with its long history of extensive use, has traditionally focused on personal characteristics that tend to link the individual to different vocational groups or environments. The thought is that effective vocational decisions probably cannot be made without a realistic assessment of one's abilities, interests, and personality. The approach, in the main, is based on the idea that human behavior can be ordered and measured along dimensions of defined traits or factors, and that individuals can be reasonably well characterized and described in terms of these defined traits. Thus the traits may be used to link people to vocational groups, and members of one vocational group will tend to have attributes different from the members of other such groups. In real life, then, this point-in-time vocational choice involves a rather direct matching of the individual's unique abilities, interests, and personality with the world's vocational opportunities. In order to assess traits (personality, abilities, interests, values, etc.), a variety of self-report tests and inventories have been developed over the years. A few examples of such tests and inventories in the ability, interest, personality, and value areas are listed below.

Special Aptitude (Ability) Tests:

Crawford Small Parts Dexterity Test—a measure of fine dexterity (wrist, finger) and manipulative skills

Purdue Pegboard—a measure of manual dexterity (arm and hand)

Revised Minnesota Paper Form Board—a measure of spatial aptitude

Minnesota Clerical Test—a measure of clerical aptitude

Meier Art Judgement Test—a measure of artistic aptitude

Seashore Measure of Musical Talents—a measure of musical aptitude

Interest Inventories:

Strong-Campbell Interest Inventory

Strong Vocational Interest Blank

Kuder Occupational Interest Survey, Form DD

Minnesota Vocational Interest Inventory for nonprofessional occupations

Self Directed Search

Personality Inventories:

Minnesota Multiphasic Personality Inventory
California Psychological Inventory
Omnibus Personality Inventory
Guilford-Zimmerman Temperament Survey
Comry Personality Scales
Cattell Sixteen Personality Questionnaire
Edwards Personal Preference Schedule

Values:

Allport, Vernon, and Lindzey Study of Values
Super's Work Values Inventory

Without question, the trait-factor approach has proved productive in advancing our knowledge and understanding of vocational behavior. However, there are concerns that the approach is too mechanistic, static, and point-in-time oriented to adequately account for vocational development. In any event, the person-centered trait approach can be beneficial if used as an additional source of information in helping people understand and think about themselves and explore various vocational possibilities and probabilities. Furthermore, there is considerable evidence indicating that individuals associated with a certain vocational group do in fact possess attributes different from the people of other vocational groups.

Super's Developmental Self-Concept Theory

Super's (1953) developmental self-concept theory revealed his commitment to developmental psychology and self-concept theory. However, his theory drew also upon the notion of individual differences and some trait-factor ideas. The key ingredient of Super's theory is the self-concept. To Super, the process of vocational development is essentially that of developing and implementing a self-concept: a person implements his or her self-concept by entering an occupation that permits self-expression. To describe vocational development, Super identified five stages: crystallization (ages 14 to 18), specification (18 to 21), implementation (21 to 24), stablization (25 to 35), and consolidation (age 35 on). The concept of vocational maturity evolved in order to assess and describe the individual's (self-concept) progress through these stages. In essence, the development of the individual's vocational self-concept is assessed according to the degree of vocational maturity (the degree of congruence between a person's vocational behavior and the expected behavior at a given age). In other words, the best way to understand future vocational behavior is to understand past vocational behavior. The vocational maturity variable has become the most applied feature of Super's theory.

To assess vocational maturity, a variety of different inventories have been developed. Crites's Career Maturity Inventory (1973) is one of the most recent and popular of these and includes an assessment of Vocational Maturity Attitude and Vocational Competence (Knowing Self, Choosing a Job, Problem Solving, Occupational Information, and Looking Ahead). Other inventories include Super's Career Questionnaire (Super, Bohn, Forrest, Jordaan, Lindeman, and Thompson, 1971), Westbrook's Cognitive Vocational Maturity Test (Westbrook and Parry-Hill, 1973), and the Readiness for Vocational Planning Scales (Gribbons and Lohnes, 1968).

In general, the evidence (Osipow, 1973) indicates that vocational maturity is a meaningful way to look at vocational development and behavior. More specifically, the evidence shows that vocational maturity tends to be associated with parental occupational level, school curriculum (college preparatory versus noncollege preparatory), amount of cultural stimulation, family cohesiveness, vocational aspirations, grades, achievement, participation in school and out-of-school activities, and independence. Vocational maturity seems to be predictive of self-improvement, occupational satisfaction, and career satisfaction. In general, the research indicates that vocational maturity is a useful predictor of vocational behavior.

Roe's Personality Theory of Career Choice

Anne Roe's theory (Roe, 1957; Roe and Klos, 1969; Roe and Siegelman, 1964) of vocational choice is based on a series of studies exploring the personalities of research scientists in different fields. The findings of these studies demonstrated differences in the personality characteristics and childhood experiences of men in different fields. Roe further concluded that a major distinction among the scientists was on a dimension of interest toward persons or not toward persons (toward things). Based on this data, Roe surmised that vocational orientation was related to personality development that was an outgrowth of early parent-child interactions.

Roe attempted to link parent-child interactions to various types of personal/vocational orientations by hypothesizing that the extent to which individuals are rewarded or punished in dealing with people or things will determine the occupational environments to which they are attracted. She thought that preferences for people activities or thing activities were probably a function of the reward or punishment pattern that developed during early parent-child interactions. For example, an individual reared in a warm and accepting family environment, in the main, has had people activities rewarded and is therefore attracted to and moves toward occupations involving frequent contact with people. On the other hand, the person raised in a cold and avoiding family environment has not been rewarded for people contact, and therefore moves toward occupations involving minimal contact with people. Person-oriented occupations are general cultural, arts and entertainment, services, and business contacts. Non-person-oriented occupations are science, outdoor, technology, and organization. The occupational groups are distributed as shown in figure 26 along two dimensions: orientation to purposeful communication to resourceful utilization, and orientation to interpersonal relation to natural phenomena. The occupational level (professional and managerial to unskilled) aspired to is based on ability and determines the amount or degree of the individual's job responsibility. The two groups of variables (occupational fields and levels) are then linked together in conical shape with the unskilled jobs in each field at the bottom of the cone, indicating that they tend to be more psychologically similar than higher level jobs. The professional and managerial jobs in each field are at the open and wide end of the cone, suggesting that such jobs in various fields tend to be more psychologically different. For example, the mechanical engineer and the actor live in very different psychological environments.

For years no attempts were made to produce within Roe's framework an empirical test or inventory for use in assessing occupational interests. More recently, however, a number of experimental inventories have been developed. Based on Roe's classification of occupations by fields and by levels, the Ramak (Meir and Barak, 1974)—meaning in Hebrew a list of occupations—was constructed. This is a list of 72 occupations which produces 24 occupational field and level scores (eight fields and three levels within each field). The California Preference System Inventory (Knapp and Knapp, 1976) was developed through factor analysis of interest-activity items written to reflect Roe's groups and levels classification. This inventory is a self-scoring and self-interpreting assessment device representing nine vocational clusters (Science, Technology, Business, Arts, Service, Consumer Economics, Outdoor, Clerical, and Comminication) at the professional and skilled levels. The Hall Occupational Orientation Inventory (Hall, 1968) is based on the development of psychological needs in occupational terms. Although the inventories are relatively new and in need of reliability and validity data, they offer promise for the future of Roe's formulations.

Research (Osipow, 1973) indicates that the psychological assumptions underlying Roe's occupational classification system are basically sound. On a more subjective basis, her classification of

Occupational Groups Ordered by Role Performers' Orientations to People, Key Data, and Natural Phenomena

Orientation to Purposeful Communication

			General Cultural	ideas		
			enlightening people			
			demonstrating mastery or principle	cooperative relations	Science "laws"	independence of relations	Outdoor nature	Orientation to Natural Phenomena
Arts & Entertainment tastes						Technology mechanics
	polite relations	sustaining people or nature			
			attending to method		
		systematizing performance			
Business Contact persuasive technique			Organization standards		
friendly relations					
Service needs	personal relations					

Orientation to Resourceful Utilization

Hypothesized horizontal dimension — Role performer's orientation to *interpersonal relations vs. natural phenomena.*

Hypothesized vertical dimension — Role performer's orientation to *purposeful communication vs. resourceful utilization.*

Hypothesized "key data" are listed near each occupational group.

Orientation to Interpersonal Relations

Figure 26. Occupational groups ordered by role performers' orientations to people, by data, and natural phenomena. *Source: A. Roe and D. Klos. Occupational Classification. The Counseling Psychologist, 1969, 1(3), 92. Copyright 1969 by the Counseling Psychologist, and reproduced with permission.*

115

occuaptional groups is very similar to Holland's derived hexagon model of occupational environments. Both Roe and Holland support with data the notion that adjacent occupational fields/environments are more closely related psychologically than distant ones. Other research (Osipow, 1973) rather clearly indicates that early social activity and experiences are related to later person orientation. Evidence shows that person-oriented students more frequently come from families where there was acceptance of and emotional concentration on the child than do nonperson-oriented students. Thus, when all is said and done, Roe's most profound applied finding is that individuals are either person or nonperson oriented in their interests and personality, and that their orientation influences to some extent the choice of an occupation.

THE ENVIRONMENTAL PERSPECTIVE

This position views behavior as mainly a function of environmental or situational factors. This perspective may be expressed as $VB = f(E)$, where E stands for the Environment or some part of the environment. Few theories of vocational development actually take this position, but a number of models that emphasize environmental characteristics have implications for vocational development and assessment. Some of these theories will be discussed here.

Barker's Behavior Setting Theory

Barker's (1968) thinking is that behavior settings (a stable pattern of activities associated with the surrounding environment) tend to shape the behavior of people who inhabit them. Behavior settings actually link actions and environments by structuring behavioral rules for specific environments or situations. The assumption is that people will tend to be influenced by the imposed behavioral rules of a setting, particularly if they obtain certain satisfaction from the setting. The thought is that in order to understand behavior, it is important to know the specific environment in which people are interacting or working.

The primary means of assessment used by Barker and his associates over the years has been the observation of people in real life. Here the assessment task involves observing the behavior of people in ongoing real-life situations or environments. To Barker, observational assessment of people in simulated or laboratory settings tends to disturb the environment and thus distort people's behavior.

The research to date has mainly focused on the differences between small settings and large settings. Settings in small organizations are assumed to be "underpersoned" and those in large organizations are assumed to be relatively "overpersoned" (there are more persons than can be accepted given the capacity of the setting). Small settings (underpersoned) have fewer people, but the same standing patterns of behavior as the large overpersoned settings. Therefore, people in small underpersoned settings are involved in more actions, stronger actions, and more varied actions in order to maintain the behavior setting. The people tend to be busier, more vigorous, more versatile, and more involved in the setting. The research (Barker, 1968; Walsh, 1973) tends to support this notion.

We find that the theory and some of the research has meaning for a broad range of environments including vocational ones. Research findings (Walsh, 1973) indicate, for example, that people working or interacting in small settings in comparison with people working in large settings are absent less often, report more satisfaction, are more productive, and evidence less turnover. In addition, people in small settings reported more group cohesiveness, greater frequency of social interaction, and easier communication than did the people in large settings. Other findings show that the smaller the work setting, the higher the morale. In small settings the work activity is reported by employees as being more meaningful, and workers perceive themselves as important to the work setting. Thus the evidence suggests in general that work settings do influence worker attitudes and behavior. People in small settings tend to be more productive, involved, and satisfied than people in large settings.

Moos's Social Ecological Approach

Moos (1976a) focuses on the social climate, suggesting that environments, like people, have unique personalities. Just as some people are more sociable and affiliative than others, so are some environments more sociable and affiliative than others. According to Moos, we should be able to describe and characterize an environment just as we describe an individual's personality. His perspective has been based on two ideas. The first is that social climate may be inferred from behavioral perceptions. Thus he describes environments as perceived by the people in them. The second idea is that the way we perceive our surroundings influences the way we behave in that environment: how the environment is perceived exerts a directional influence on behavior; the social climate tends to shape behavior and people. Or, in our context, the social climate in which one works tends to have a significant impact on attitudes, behavior, and physical and psychological well-being.

The work of Moos (1976a) and others indicates that very different social environments may be described by some common sets of dimensions associated with three somewhat global categories. These categories of dimensions are the Relationship dimensions, the Personal Development dimensions, and the System Maintenance and System Change dimensions. The Relationship dimensions assess the amount of person involvement in the environment, the degree to which they support each other, and the amount of spontaneity or expression among the people in the environment. Some common Relationship dimensions are Involvement, Cohesiveness, Emotional Support, Peer Cohesion, Staff Support, Expressiveness, and Spontaneity. The Personal Development dimensions assess the potential in the environment for personal growth and the development of self-esteem. Specific dimensions are Independence, Intellectual-Cultural Orientation, Moral-Religious Emphasis, Competition, Autonomy, and Practical Orientation. The System Maintenance and Change dimensions assess the extent to which the environment is orderly, clear in its expectations, and responsive to change. Common basic dimensions are Order and Organization, Clarity, Control, and Innovation. A significant feature of identifying some common dimensions across different social environments is that such environments may now be compared and attempts may be made to explore why an individual does well in one environment and not so well in another.

To make the above dimensions real and characterize social environments, Moos and his colleagues have developed a number of perceived climate scales. For example, perceived-climate scales used to measure treatment environments are the Ward Atmosphere Scale (Moos, 1976b) and the Community Oriented Programs Environment Scale (Moos, 1976c). A Climate scale used to measure institutional environments is the Correctional Institutions Environment Scale (Moos, 1976d). Scales used to assess educational environments are the University Residence Environment Scale (Moos and Gerst, 1976) and the Classroom Environment Scale (Moos and Truckett, 1976). Finally, scales used to assess community environments are the Work Environments Scale (Moos and Insel, 1976), the Group Environment Scale (Moos and Humphrey, 1976), and the Family Environment Scale (Moos, 1976e).

Some of the research clearly has implications for vocational assessment, choice, and satisfaction. For example, considerable evidence (Moos, 1976a) shows that the quality of personal interaction with supervisors in work environments is associated with job satisfaction and performance. Workers who perceived their work environment as supportive were rated more favorably by their supervisors on dimensions of competence, friendliness, and conscientiousness. Some findings on life insurance agents and their managers have shown that general satisfaction with the work environment was related to Relationship, Personal Development, and System Maintenance dimensions. Research exploring the intentions of bank customers revealed that customers who perceived the bank employees to be friendly and supportive were least likely to switch accounts. Customers who switched accounts perceived the bank and its personnel less favorably than did those who maintained their accounts. In another research area of interest, some evidence (Moos, 1976a) suggests that the perceived social environment has important physiological and health-related effects. Specifically, work pressure and too much responsibility tend to be associated with higher cardiac rates and cardiac problems. In general, the evidence suggests that people who are satisfied in jobs have a much better chance of remaining healthy than those who are not.

Overall, the evidence does suggest that social environments do tend to shape behavior. In the main, workers tend to be more productive and satisfied in environments that are relationship oriented (affiliative, supportive, and expressive). Furthermore, workers are less likely to drop out and be absent. Order and clarity have a limited positive effect on worker satisfaction and performance. However, increased responsibility and work pressure tend to have a negative effect on physical and psychological well-being. In sum, the information to date indicates that perceived environments have impact on the worker's coping behavior, physiological health, and psychological well-being.

SUMMARY

This chapter has been devoted to some discussion of various theoretical perspectives of vocational psychology that people may use to assess and organize information about themselves. The theories assuming an interactional perspective have suggested that vocational development is a function of the person and the environment; their notion is that assessment of the person is incomplete without some assessment of the environment. Theories assuming the person perspective have focused on the individual's personal characteristics as the primary determinant of vocational behavior; it is individual personality that links the person to a vocational environment. The environment perspective suggests that vocational behavior is a function of environment or context variables; the context is the determining variable and the individual's behavior tends to vary from one context or environment to another. Within these three perspectives, the theories discussed seem to be the most meaningful for helping people assess, organize, and understand information about themselves and their social environments.

Applications
of Tests
and Measurements

TESTS AND INDIVIDUAL DECISIONS

Tests are tools designed to be used in making human decisions. In our complex, many-faceted society, thousands of decisions that involve some evaluation of a person's psychological characteristics are made every day. Some are decisions people make in planning their own lives, as when Jerry makes up his mind to enter graduate school instead of taking a job as a petroleum geologist, or when Juanita signs up for the Women's Job Corps. Some are decisions people make about others, as when Mr. Christie decides which of three applicants to hire as a secretary, or Dr. Ludwig and his colleagues in a mental health clinic plan the treatment of a new patient. In any of these situations, a well chosen test in the hands of someone who understands it may be of enormous value.

Personal Decisions

As emphasized in previous chapters, the utilization of test information is complicated by the fact that no test is a completely valid measure of a given psychological characteristic, and that a score is inevitably a somewhat inaccurate measure of anything—in other words, that the validity and reliability of any test is less than perfect. This is why testing and counseling programs often go together. Talking test results over with someone who thoroughly understands what one can and cannot conclude from them leads to sounder decisions than does accepting scores at face value.

In struggling with the problem of whether to take the job as an oil company geologist or return to graduate school to work for a Ph.D., for example, Jerry may wish to compare his general intellectual ability with that of other graduate students by means of a test like the Graduate Record Examination. But how shall he use the information that his score is 450? If norm tables tell him that this is just a little below the average level for graduate students in geology, he cannot be certain of below-average grades. Tabulations of what students in the past have done show that some students with scores like his come out with straight A's, others with C minus averages. Which kind is he? Error in either direction in his decision will be costly to him. If he decides to go ahead with graduate work and finds after a year or two that he is not going to be able to qualify for a Ph.D., he will feel that he has wasted a considerable fraction of his life. Further, he may not at that time have as good a position offered him as the oil company is offering him now. If, on the other hand, he decides *against* graduate work on the basis of his below-average score, he may be cutting himself off for the rest of his life from the highest levels of his profession, levels that at least *some* persons with scores like his reach. If Jerry is to make a good decision here, he must consider many factors. His test score is only one.

A test that is to play a part in vital decisions should be chosen very carefully. While it should be *reliable* enough to provide a fairly accurate indication of an individual's relative standing in terms of the characteristics measured, the really important consideration is *predictive validity*. We must know what kind of progress, along specified lines, research has shown can be expected of persons with low, medium, and high scores. A testing tool to be used in decision making is not built all at once like a house or a machine. It *develops* over a period of years, and its usefulness *grows* as experience with it increases. We could range all the varieties of tests we have considered along a scale that would show how well developed they are at present. A brand-new test, no matter how ingenious an idea it represents or how great the social need for it, would be at the bottom of such a "development" scale. A test like the Stanford-Binet, which has been in continuous use since 1916, would stand at the top, for a well-trained examiner familiar with the large body of knowledge that has grown up around it knows what this test measures and what kinds of decisions it facilitates.

However, there is a place for new tests in counseling, where they can sometimes prove fruitful sources of ideas for counselor and counselee to check out against nontest evidence. In such cases, however, it is especially important that the counselor know enough to make clear which kinds of test results cannot stand alone.

Another practical point to be noted when test results enter into personal decisions is that low scores may be significant even if high scores are not—and vice versa. To go back to Jerry and his thinking about graduate school, if he finds out that 500 is the minimum level for acceptance into the graduate schools he considers to have excellent geology programs, it is clear that regardless of how many other assets he may have, his GRE score of 450 disqualifies him. Had his score been 650, however, he might have had no advantage over another applicant with a score of 550, since beyond a certain level of general intellectual ability, success in graduate work depends upon other qualities of mind and character than academic aptitude. Information like this constitutes part of the background a person needs in order to interpret test results intelligently. Just knowing reliability and validity coefficients does not suffice.

This discussion of some of the less obvious points to be considered in using test information for self-evaluation is related to a controversial issue that has arisen again and again down through the years. Should children be told what their IQ's are? On the one hand, it is claimed that they and their parents have a right to know, so that the plans and decisions they make, particularly with regard to continued education, may be appropriate. On the other hand, it is argued that a single IQ figure, without the background we have been considering, is likely to be misinterpreted and lead to plans that do not work out well. Probably the most justifiable policy for a school to adopt is to make test results available to students and their parents but to be sure to provide interpretive information along with them. It is doubtful whether a school can benefit from a testing program unless there are people on the staff who understand tests and their limitations. School counselors often serve in this capacity.

Decisions About Other People

The kinds of decision about other people for which tests have most commonly been used in the past are *selection* decisions. When one's job is to select one or more individuals from among a group of applicants, the contribution a test makes can be analyzed in a simple straightforward way. Whether the selection is for a college, for a job, or for a therapy group, the purpose of the decision maker is to pick out people who will *fit into the place in mind for them.* The decision maker does not expect to be right every time, only most of the time—he or she wants to select more successes than failures. Tests can sometimes improve one's batting average even if their reliability and predictive validity are not especially high. Consider, for example, the expectancy table shown in Table 6. If the personnel woman who does the hiring selects only those applicants who make scores of 14 or higher on the test, she can expect that all of them will succeed and none of them really fail. In a tight labor market, she may have to hire people who get scores lower than 12 in order to get enough workers to keep things going. In this case, though, she anticipates that there will be a larger number of failures, but still not as many as there would have been if no test had been used. For her a test is mainly a tool to use in increasing the *number* of successes, and lessening the *number* of failures. She is not concerned about the meaning of individual scores and patterns of scores. She realizes that some errors in selection occur as the test is used—that some persons with high scores do not do well—but she does not worry about these failures as long as there are not too many of them. Another possible

Table 6

How a Stenographic Proficiency Test Can Contribute
to the Selection of Good Stenographers

NUMBER IN EACH SCORE GROUP RECEIVING EACH RATING ON STENOGRAPHIC ABILITY				Stenographic Proficiency Test Scores	PERCENTAGE IN EACH RATING GROUP THAT FALL IN EACH SCORE GROUP			
Below Average	Average	Above Average	Excellent		Below Average	Average	Above Average	Excellent
	4	6	7	18-19		17	40	64
	2	2	4	16-17		9	13	36
	10	5		14-15		44	33	
	4	1		12-13		17	7	
2	2	1		10-11	67	9	7	
1	1			8-9	33	4		
3	23	15	11		100	100	100	100

This expectancy table shows the number and percentage of stenographers of various rated abilities who came from specified score groups on the *S-B Stenographic Proficiency Test.* ($N = 52$, mean score = 15.4, S.D. = 2.9, r = .61; score is average per letter for five letters.) It indicates that if only girls who scored at least 14 had been hired, none of them would have been rated "below average" and many would have been rated "above average" or "superior." (From Psychological Corporation *Test Service Bulletin*, No. 38, New York, 1949.)

error does not bother her at all—that because of low test scores she may have turned down a few persons who might have been outstanding successes.

However, increasing numbers of people have begun to worry about the long-range effects upon society as a whole of the standard way tests have been used in selection decisions. The personnel manager may not be concerned about low scorers who might have been successful on the job had they been hired, but society is. Many of the so-called hard-core unemployed are persons who have been rejected again and again because they never scored near the top of any distribution of test scores, in school or in employment offices. It is becoming clear that our selection procedures do not result in putting everybody to work.

It is possible that the most important result of our increasing concern about the indirect effects of testing on society will be a conceptual shift from a *selection* system to a *classification* system of thinking about personnel decisions. If instead of the question, Is this person to be accepted or rejected? we ask, Where will this person best fit in?, most of the difficulties we have been discussing disappear. Many progressive companies are experimenting with plans under which they will hire anyone who wishes to work, and then use all of the resources of professional personnel administration to reach a decision about what job or training program will suit him best. Employment agencies often operate in this way, especially those making a special effort to serve the young, the inexperienced, or the disadvantaged.

The diagnostic decisions for which tests are used in clinics can also be considered to be classification rather than selection. The basic question is, "Just what is *wrong* here?" When a mentally ill patient enters a hospital, the first step is to try to find out what the patient is suffering from. If general symptoms suggest either schizophrenia or an organic psychosis arising from a brain disease, the psychologist uses tests that previous research has shown differentiate between schizophrenic and organic patients. Since such diagnostic decisions are typically made by teams of experts rather than by a psychologist alone, the clues obtained from testing are supplemented by clues coming from other types of examination. In this case, an analysis of the patient's electroencephalogram (a record of electrical activity in the brain) and a physician's report about the patient's illnesses that might have produced brain damage would almost certainly be brought in. Tests are also used in this diagnostic way by reading specialists who try to pinpoint a slow reader's trouble so that they can teach the individual material not learned in the regular schoolroom, by speech therapists who suspect that personality characteristics are relevant in the case of a stutterer, and by many other clinical and educational workers.

Such clinical uses differ from the employment situations discussed above in that test results need only furnish clues or hypotheses, which are always checked against other kinds of information about the person being studied. Thus, it is even more true here than in employment situations that tests may be of some value even though they are not highly reliable or completely valid for the purpose for which the examiner is using them. The psychologist's ingenuity in thinking of ways to track down new clues about the patient's difficulty is what counts. The psychologist may even improvise some testing procedures that have never been studied systematically at all. If such procedures furnish hypotheses the examiner can check against facts drawn from the patient's behavior, symptoms, and history, they have served their purpose. But that some novel, unstandardized procedure is a workable test in a particular case (or even in 10 or 100 cases) does not constitute evidence that is a useful tool for decision making in *all* comparable situations. In fact, many instruments used in diagnostic testing do not meet the standards we set up in Chapter 3. This charge applies to a large proportion of the projective tests in clinical use. Therefore, we must be careful not to conclude that they would be valuable when decisions are made entirely or mainly on the basis of test results alone. It is imperative that hypotheses based on tests that are less then adequate be checked against other sources of information.

Tests and Decisions: Some General Considerations

Clearly, the standards we apply in selecting tests should be determined by the use we plan to make of the results. We can never say, "This is the *best* intelligence test; go ahead and use it for everything," or "This is a *good* test of emotional maturity." We always ask, "*Who* is to use the results of this test, and for *what* purposes?"

Whenever possible, one should *try out* a proposed test in a particular situation where one expects to use it. After we find out how the testees in this trial group perform, we can set up expectancy tables like the one shown in Table 6, or work our regression equations for predictive purposes based on this group. If, for example, an insurance company that has hired very few black office workers in the past decides to increase the number, a preliminary study is advisable, in which all applicants are given the clerical ability test the company has been using, but hired without reference to test results. After perhaps 6 months, the performance of these clerks can be checked against their test scores. This will show how many failures there were altogether and how many of these would have been eliminated by the setting of a particular passing score that would have disqualified some applicants at the outset (and also how many who turned out to be satisfactory workers would have been disqualified and not given a chance to show how good they really were). Too often, extensive testing programs have been set up without such preliminary tryouts and have led to unsound decisions about people.

It is often useful to plan preliminary studies so as to compare the utilities of several tests rather than simply to evaluate one. It is also advisable, if one's orientation is classification rather than selection, to plan a preliminary study that includes applicants for several different jobs, rather than just one. In the example given in the previous paragraph, five short tests might have been used to select black clerical workers for positions as stenographers, bookkeepers, card punchers, and file clerks.

Persons responsible for deciding whether to use tests or not in a particular personnel situation must often weigh the expense of a testing program against the cost of training. If a job calls for a skill anyone can learn in a few days, using tests to select particularly apt persons is usually not worthwhile. On the other hand, if long training periods and costly equipment are needed to make a person skillful, as in the case of airplane pilots, even a very expensive testing program can be justified if it contributes materially to the selection of candidates who are ultimately successful.

Making judgments about people is a complex process. Tests are tools to be used by those whose job it is to make such judgments. Tests do not make decisions for us. They cannot stand alone. If we always keep this fact in mind we will reap the benefits of psychological testing without stumbling into any of the pitfalls that present themselves.

TESTS AS RESEARCH TOOLS

In Chapter One the point was made that measurement is essential to psychological research. Measurement, of course, is a broad term including many other procedures as well as those we ordinarily call tests. Let us now look briefly at the question, How are tests used to advance psychological knowledge?

Individual Differences

The research area most closely linked to mental testing is differential psychology, the study of the differences between human individuals. In addition to designing instruments that serve useful purposes in schools, clinics, and personnel offices, psychologists have proposed theories and carried on investigations to test them out—theories about the nature of intelligence, the structure of mental abilities, the origins of sex differences, the relationship of mental to physical characteristics, to name just a few.

One of the most valuable legacies these investigators have left to the researchers now studying human differences is a clarification of the distinction between profitable and unprofitable questions. At the beginning, the questions they asked were broad and inclusive. Are intelligence differences the result of heredity or environment? Are men more intelligent than women? Do the races differ in intelligences? Is the IQ constant? Is the human race more variable in psychological characteristics than in physical characteristics? Is the mental capacity of the human race declining? Do differences between individuals increase or decrease with practice?

As time passed, it became apparent that for various reasons mental tests were not going to provide answers to questions like these. Some problems, such as the comparison of variability in human intelligence to variability in height were seen to be insoluble because of the scale properties of test scores, as soon as such properties were understood. Height is measured on a *ratio* scale (see Chapter One) so that it is legitimate to say that the tallest adult ever measured is about three times as tall as the shortest. But intelligence is not measured on a ratio scale so that dividing one IQ by another produces a meaningless index. Thus, with the kind of mental tests we have, we cannot compare human variability in mental traits to that in physical traits.

For other questions, such as comparisons of the sexes, the races, or the social classes, the problem is the *content* of the tests we use to measure mental characteristics. The tests permit us to make valid comparisons between individuals *within* one of these social groups because we can assume that the experience of all of those tested has been similar enough to make the test score mainly a reflection of the quality of the individual's thinking rather than of some peculiarity in his background. When we compare the averages of groups for whom we know experience with problems and questions like those in the test has not been similar—blacks and whites, for example—we simply do not know what the results mean. Although typically whites score higher on intelligence tests, we cannot conclude that the white race is superior. We cannot conclude either, on the basis of mental test evidence, that the races are equal. We simply cannot conclude anything at all. The only sensible course is to drop the question.

At one time it was thought that culture-free or culture-fair tests would open the matter up again, but the progress of research has dampened these hopes. To present test questions in the form of pictures rather than words does not solve the problem, because looking at pictures is now known to be a learned skill, and in some cultures children do not typically acquire it. To ask subjects to deal with geometrical forms rather than with objects of common use does not solve the problem because perceiving shapes is also a learned skill. People who live in round houses and spend their days in fields or forests do not learn to discriminate angles and rectangles.

It appears now that it is better to revise the research questions, casting them in a narrower, more limited mold, than to attempt to develop testing methods to answer the broad questions. If we take as an example the question that has probably interested more people than any other in differential psychology, the relative influence of heredity and environment on individual differences in intelligence, we can see how a program of research on more limited questions has led to dependable although far from complete knowledge. We have established that there are intellectual differences based on heredity, even though we do not have pure measures of them.

The most significant findings have come out of studies of *twins*. Identical, or *monozygotic*, twins are ideal subjects for research on heredity, because they have identical sets of genes. In such cases, the two individuals have grown from a single fertilized egg cell that separated into parts at the time of the first cell division. Thus, any differences in behavior, ability, or personality between such twins must be based on some environmental influence. It cannot be hereditary.

In twin studies, two research designs are most commonly used. The first is to compare the amount of resemblance in identical twin pairs with the amount of resemblance in other pairs of children. The first step is to find out how much alike the identical twin pairs are, on the average, in some characteristic, such as intelligence. The next step is to see how much alike fraternal, or *dizygotic*, twins are (those growing out of two fertilized egg cells, and thus no more alike in their gene pattern than any two siblings are). Often a third step is added—to see how much alike non-twin siblings are. Because resemblances between children in the same family can arise from either heredity or environment, or from both, the comparisons of different kinds of sibling pairs enable us to sort out some of these determiners and draw some tentative conclusions about whether or not any particular trait has a hereditary basis. If it has, we would expect identical twins to resemble each other most closely because both heredity and environment are likely to affect them in similar ways. Siblings of different ages would be the least similar, since some of the family environmental influences on their development would be dissimilar because of the time lapse between one child and the other. Fraternal twins should be somewhere in between, since they are no more alike in heredity than ordinary siblings are, but they do experience the family environment at the same time. For intelligence, this is, in fact, exactly what we find, as shown in Figure 27. Since this pattern of correlations is highly similar to that for height and other physical characteristics known to be determined principally by heredity, it seems reasonable to conclude that differences in intelligence also are based on heredity. A similar pattern has been found for some of the special abilities, such as mechanical and motor skills, and for some personality deviations, such as schizophrenia.

Other more recent findings from the National Merit study (Lochlin and Nichols, 1976) and the Louisville Twin Study (Wilson, 1977) are supportive of the above conclusion. The National Merit study using 850 pairs of twins found that identical twins were more alike than fraternal twins on just about any ability or personality trait. However, the authors point out that according to their findings no one cognitive or personality variable is more heritable than any other. The longitudinal Louisville Twin Study which has been following 157 pairs of twins that are now of school age recently evalu-

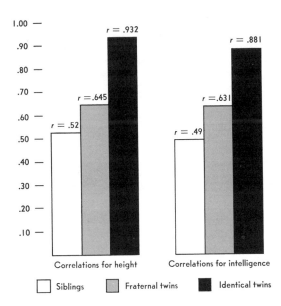

Figure 27. Correlations between pairs of children in the same family for height and for intelligence. *(Twin correlations from R. S. Woodworth. Heredity and Environment. Soc. Sci. Res. Council, New York, 1941. Sibling correlations from H. S. Conrad and H. E. Jones. Yearbook Nat. Soc. Stud. Educ. 39 (1940). II: 97–141; and K. Pearson and A. Lee. Biometrika. 2 (1903): 357–462.)*

ated the intelligence variable using the Wechsler Intelligence Scale for Children. The findings again were consistent with our above discussion indicating substantial genetic influence on the trait of intellegence.

The twin method has been sufficiantly productive to generate interest in exploring its use with a range of other variables such as academic abilities, vocational interests, creative abilities, language, reading, and social attitudes. The popularity and success of the twin method suggests that it will continue to be a valuable method for collecting meaningful information pertaining to individual differences.

The second design in twin research involves comparing the resemblance between identical twins reared together with the resemblance between identical twins reared apart. Figure 28 illustrates what has been found. If heredity were *all*-important in determining an individual's intelligence or other psychological characteristics, it would be irrelevant whether identical twins were brought up in the same home and community or not. If environment were *all*-important, identical twins reared apart would be no more alike than random pairs of children. The principal reason we now know that neither of these extreme statements is true in the case of intelligence and a number of other mental characteristics is that research points to a reality somewhere between the two extremes. As Figure 28 shows, the average difference between twins *is* greater for those reared apart than for those reared together, but it is nowhere nearly as great as the difference between unrelated children.

It is these studies of identical twins reared in different homes and communities that have told us most about what *aspect* of the environment has the greatest effect on intelligence. In a thorough

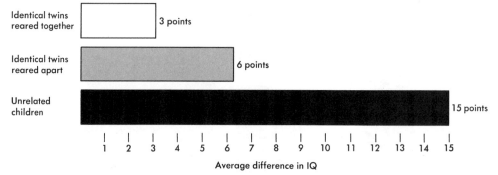

Figure 28. Average IQ differences for pairs of children with different degrees of relationship. *(From R. S. Woodworth. Heredity and Environment. Soc. Sci. Res. Council, New York, 1941.)*

case study of nineteen pairs of separated identical twins, H. H. Newman rated the environments separately for the educational and social advantages they provided. In all instances where one twin turned out to be much brighter than another, educational influences differed markedly. But social advantages did not seem to have much effect.

Other questions about the relative hereditary or environmental determination of various psychological characteristics have been approached in several other ways—studies of family histories, research on children in foster homes, animal-breeding studies. All these lines of investigation point to the general conclusion that many or most abilities and personality traits have some hereditary basis, but that their development is also affected by environmental influences.

Researchers are now looking closely at specific kinds of environmental influences, attempting to find out how they influence development. During the 1960s, for example, there had been a great deal of interest in *early* education, the learning preschool children do, upon which later learning depends. Susan W. Gray and Rupert A. Klaus, an example of whose findings appears in Figure 29, have shown that the rate of mental growth for groups undergoing a carefully planned preschool experience is significantly higher than the rate for groups not given this education. How lasting the acceleration is in later years is another specific research question on which information is being obtained by these investigators and by others in several places.

Research on individual differences is increasingly turning out to be research on human *development*. The knowledge that would be most useful in planning improvements in society would have to do with particular kinds of influence to be applied at certain stages of development in specified situations. We are making progress in accumulating this knowledge. Mental tests serve as indices of how the development of individuals is proceeding, and thus play a prominent part in such research undertakings.

Experimental Research

For many years after the testing movement began, the psychologists carrying out observational and correlational studies constituted one branch of scientific psychology, and those carrying out experiments in laboratories constituted another. There was very little interaction. Correlational psychologists used tests; experimental psychologists typically used other kinds of measurements. The main distinction between the two approaches to research is that an experi-

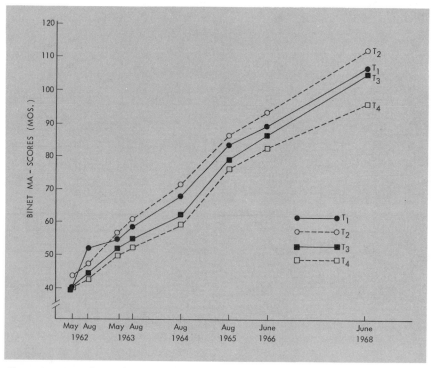

Figure 29. Mental growth curved over a 6 year period for two preschool groups (T₁ and T₂) and two control groups (T₃ and T₄). *(From Rupert A. Klaus and Susan W. Gray, unpublished manuscript, by permission.)*

mentalist *manipulates* the independent variables. He provides the stimulus conditions to which the subject is to respond and measures the effects of changes in these conditions.

As long as laboratory researchers were interested in the less complex aspects of learning, motivation, and performance, simple measurements of behavior sufficed—things like the number of errors a rat made in traversing a maze or the number of milliseconds a person took to depress a key in response to a signal. But with the increasing application of experimental methods to problems in human thinking, personality, and social behavior, the need for measures of complex human characteristics became apparent, and the experimenters turned to tests of intelligence, special abilities, achievement, and personality. More and more psychologists crossed the invisible line that had formerly kept laboratory researchers and mental testers apart.

The most frequent use of tests in psychological experiments is as *dependent* variables. One may be interested, for example, in the effects of drugs on intelligence test performance, or in the effects of stress on measured self-confidence. Tests may also be used as *control* variables. One may wish to find out, for example, what effect different kinds of instructions have on problem solving, and start by dividing the subjects into high, average, and low groups on the basis of an intelligence test.

Tests that are used to measure variables in a psychological or educational experiment must be evaluated somewhat differently than tests designed to contribute to individual decision making. In many instances new or inadequately developed tests can serve a very useful purpose in experiments. It is not important, for one thing, that good *norms* be provided by the author or publishers of the test if the experimenter is not interested in the general level of ability and achievement shown by his subjects, but only in whether the experimental group scores higher than the control group. Validity considerations may not be very important if the experimenter only plans to use the results as a means of testing out some theoretical hypothesis. It is not important that the test to be used have a high reliability coefficient if only group averages are to be compared. Chance errors will tend to cancel each other out, leaving a fairly accurate average figure even if individual scores are inaccurate.

Besides the limitation on what can be done with numbers that do not constitute a ratio scale, there is one other special complication that must be kept in mind when tests are used in experimental research. This is the fact that it is difficult if not impossible to measure *change* satisfactorily by means of psychological tests. No problem arises if the research question is of the simple Yes or No variety, such as "Did the training in perceptual discrimination produce a significant increase in IQ?" But investigators ran into trouble in experiments designed to compare the *change* resulting from one treatment with the *change* resulting from another. One source of the difficulty is what is called the *ceiling* effect. Most tests are made up of questions to be answered, and persons who at the outset already know most of the right answers are able to demonstrate very little gain, regardless of how much the experimental situation changes them. Another root of the problem is *unreliability*. If the initial score each experimental subject makes is inaccurate because of chance errors (and all test scores are, to some extent, as has been explained) and the final score the subject makes is also inaccurate, subtracting one from the other produces a figure with a "double dose" of unreliability. Subject X, for example, may have happened to score somewhat higher than he or she should have the first time around, and somewhat lower the second time. This makes it *appear* that the change produced by the experiment is negligible or even in the wrong direction. Subject Y, on the other hand, was unlucky the first time, and lucky the second. This makes for what *looks like* a large positive increment. The unwary experimenter may conclude that Y has learned much more than X, even though no real difference at all exists.

Various ways have been proposed for avoiding the pitfalls to which change scores lead. The simplest and most satisfactory is to design the experiment so that it is not necessary to use change scores at all. If several kinds of experimental treatment are to be tried out, individuals from the total pool of subjects can be *randomly* assigned to Group A, Group B, Group C, etc. Comparing the average scores these groups make on the test at the end of the experiment will then answer the research question directly, since there is no reason to believe that any systematic difference between the groups existed at the outset.

APPLICATIONS OF TESTS AND MEASUREMENTS—A FINAL WORD

The quantification of human traits, the invention of statistical methods appropriate for the kinds of numbers obtained, the construction of tests to measure abilities and personality characteristics—all these tasks have called for ingenuity, clear thinking, and a dash of cautious skepticism. The same qualities are needed by those who would use tests and measurements profitably. They are human tools designed for human purposes. By themselves they settle no theoretical arguments, treat no patients, educate no children, solve no social problems. But in the hands of skilled workers who understand them they can help us in all these undertakings. Each individual is required to make decisions about many matters related to work and other people. Dozens of social problems cry out for solutions. How sound these decisions and solutions are will depend to a large extent on the care and creativity of the decision makers and the investigators, those who evaluate people and who plan and carry out programs of basic research. It is the contribution tests and measurements make to these significant undertakings that justifies their existence.

Selected Readings

ANASTASI, ANNE. *Psychological Testing*. 4th ed. New York: Macmillan Publishing Co., 1976.

> This is another good survey of the whole field of psychological testing.

ANASTASI, ANNE, ed. *Testing Problems in Perspective*. Washington: American Council on Education, 1966.

> In 1936 the American Council on Education inaugurated a series of annual invitational conferences on testing problems. This book is a 25th anniversary volume that brings together many of the major issues and ideas participants discussed.

BUROS, E. K. Jr., ed. *Mental Measurements Yearbook*. Highland Park, N. J.: Gryphon Press.

> There have been seven editions of this indispensable reference book in the years from 1941 to 1972. In each of them, essential information about each particular test is summarized, and two or more reviewers comment on its strengths and weaknesses.

CRONBACH, LEE J. *Essentials of Psychological Testing*. 3rd ed. New York: Harper & Row, Publishers, 1970.

> This is one of the best complete surveys of the whole field of psychological testing. Additional information about any of the tests mentioned in the present book is presented, and a great many other tests are discussed in some detail.

GUILFORD, J. P. *Intelligence, Creativity and their Educational Implications*. San Diego, Calif.: Robert R. Knapp, 1968.

> Guilford has been one of the most outstanding contributors to measurement theory and technique. This book will introduce the student to some of his ideas.

HAMMOND, KENNETH R., and JAMES E. HOUSEHOLDER. *Introduction to the Statistical Method.* New York: Alfred A. Knopf, Inc., 1962.

> In this book a psychologist and mathematician have combined their efforts to present the basic ideas of statistics in an exceptionally lucid and interesting way.

HUNT, J. McV. *Intelligence and Experience.* New York: The Ronald Press Company, 1961.

> To date, this is the best synthesis of a large amount of research designed to show what intelligence is and how it grows.

OSIPOW, S. H. *Theories of Career Development.* 2nd ed. New York: Appleton-Century-Crofts, 1973.

> This is a comprehensive review of most of the theories of career development discussed in the present volume.

PETERSON, JOSEPH. *Early Conceptions and Tests of Intelligence.* Yonkers: World Book, 1925.

> The early history of intelligence testing is covered here in much more detail than in other texts. It is often interesting for the student to understand the thinking of the people who began the work in a major area.

TYLER, LEONA E. *The Psychology of Human Differences.* New York: Appleton-Century-Crofts, 1965.

> In this more extensive book, many of the ideas discussed briefly in the present volume are gone into in more detail, with research evidence.

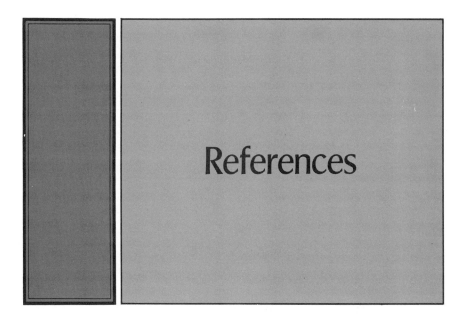

References

Astin, A. W. and J. L. Holland, "The Environmental Assessment Technique: A way to measure college environments," *Journal of Educational Psychology 52* (1961), 308-316.

Barker, R. G., *Ecological psychology: Concepts and methods for studying the environment of human behavior.* Stanford, California: Stanford University Press, 1968.

Bohn, M. J., Jr., "Psychological needs related to personality types," *Journal of Counseling Psychology 13* (1966), 306-309.

Campbell, D. J. and D. W. Fiske, "Convergent and discriminant validation by the multitrait-multimethod matrix," *Psychological Bulletin, 56* (1959), 81-105.

Campbell, D. P., *Manual for the SVIB-SCII Strong-Campbell Interest Inventory* (2nd edition). Stanford, California: Stanford University Press, 1977.

Cohen, R. D., *Students and colleges: Need-press dimensions for the development of a common framework for characterizing students and colleges.* (Ed 01 1083) Washington: U.S. Office of Education, September, 1966.

Crites, J. O., *Career Maturity Inventory: Theory and research handbook and administration and use manual.* Del Monte Research Park, California: CTB McGraw-Hill, 1973.

Gribbons, W. B. and P. R. Lohnes, *Emerging careers.* New York: Teachers College Press, 1968.

Hall, L. G. *Hall Occupation Orientation Inventory.* Chicago: Follett, 1968.

Hathaway, S. R. and J. C. McKinley, *Manual for the Minnesota Multiphasic Personality Inventory.* New York: The Psychological Corporation, 1967.

137

Holland, J. H., *Making vocational choices: A theory of careers.* Englewood Cliffs, N. J.: Prentice-Hall, 1973.

——*Manual for the Vocational Preference Inventory.* Palo Alto, Calif.: Consulting Psychologists Press, 1975.

—— *Professional manual for the Self-Directed Search.* Palo Alto, Calif.: Consulting Psychologists Press, 1972.

Holland, J. L., *Making vocational choices: A theory of careers.* Englewood Cliffs, N.J.: Prentice-Hall, 1973.

Holland, J. L. and G. D. Gottfredson, "Using a typology of person and environments to explain careers: Some extensions and clarifications," *Counseling Psychologist* 6 (1976), 20-29.

Knapp, R. R. and L. Knapp, *The California Occupational Preference System, Technical Manual.* San Diego, California: EDITS, 1976.

Kuder, G. F., *Manual, Kuder Occupational Interest Survey, Form DD.* Chicago: Science Research Association, 1968.

Lewin, K., *Principles of topological psychology.* New York: McGraw Hill, 1936.

Loehlin, J. C. and R. C. Nichols, *Heredity, environment and personality.* Austin: University of Texas Press, 1976.

Meir, E. I. and A. Barak, "A simple instrument for measuring vocational interests based on Roe's classification of occupations," *Journal of Vocational Behavior* 4 (1974), 33-42.

Moos, R. H., *The human context.* New York: John Wiley, 1976 (a).

—— *Community Oriented Program Environment Scales Manual.* Palo Alto, California: Consulting Psychologists Press, 1976 (b).

—— *Correctional Institution Environment Scale Manual.* Palo Alto, California: Consulting Psychologists Press, 1976 (c).

—— *Family Environment Scale Manual.* Palo Alto, California: Consulting Psychologists Press, 1976 (d).

—— *Ward Atmosphere Scale Manual.* Palo Alto, California: Consulting Psychologists Press, 1976 (e).

——, and M. Gerst, *University Residence Environment Scale Manual.* Palo Alto, California: Consulting Psychologists Press, 1976.

Moos, R. H. and B. Humphrey, *Group Environment Scale Manual.* Palo Alto, California: Consulting Psychologists Press, 1976.

Moos, R. H. and R. Insel, *Work Environment Scale Manual.* Palo Alto, California: Consulting Psychologists Press, 1976.

Moos, R. H. and E. Trickett, *Classroom Environment Scale Manual.* Palo Alto, California: Consulting Psychologists Press, 1976.

Murray, H. A., *Explorations in personality.* New York: Oxford University Press, 1938.

Neff, W. S., *Work and human behavior.* New York: Atherton, 1968.

Osipow, S. H., *Theories of Career Development,* (2nd ed.) Englewood Cliffs, N.J.: Prentice-Hall, 1973.

Roe, A., "Early determinants of vocational choice," *Journal of Counseling Psychology* 4 (1957), 212-217.

Roe, A. and D. Klos, "Occupational classification," *The Counseling Psychologist 1* (1969), 84-92.

Roe, A. and M. Siegelman, *The origin of interests*. The APGA Inquiry Series, No. 1, Washington D.C.: American Personnel and Guidance Association, 1964.

Standards for educational and psychological tests. Washington, D.C.: American Psychological Association, 1974.

Standards for educational and psychological tests and manuals. Washington, D.C.: American Psychological Association, 1966.

Stern, G. G., *People in context*. New York: Wiley, 1970.

Stevens, S. S., *Handbook of experimental psychology*. New York: John Wiley, 1951.

Super, D. E., "A theory of vocational development," *American Psychologist*, 8 (1953), 185-190.

Super, D. E.; M. J. Bohn, Jr.; D. J. Forrest; J. P. Jordaan; R. L. Lindeman; and A. S. Thompson, *Career Questionnaire Form IV*. New York: Teachers College, Columbia University, 1971.

Technical recommendations for achievement tests. Washington, D.C.: American Educational Research Association, 1955.

Walsh, W. B., *Theories of person-environment interaction: Implications for the college student*. The American College Testing Program, 1973.

Westbrook, B. W., and J. W. Parry-Hill, Jr., "The measure of cognitive vocational maturity," *Journal of Vocational Behavior, 3* (1973), 239-252.

Wilson, R. S. Twins and siblings: Concordance for school-age mental development. *Child Development, 48* (1977), 211-216.

Zytowski, D. G., "The effects of being interest inventoried," *Journal of Vocational Behavior*, 1977, 11, 153-158.

Zytowski, D. G., "Predictive validity of the Kuder Occupational Interest Survey: A 12-to-19 year follow-up," *Journal of Counseling Psychology, 23*, (1976), 221-233.

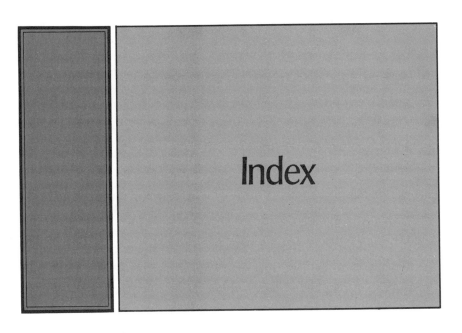

Index